Communications
in Computer and Information Science　　1276

Commenced Publication in 2007
Founding and Former Series Editors:
Simone Diniz Junqueira Barbosa, Phoebe Chen, Alfredo Cuzzocrea,
Xiaoyong Du, Orhun Kara, Ting Liu, Krishna M. Sivalingam,
Dominik Ślęzak, Takashi Washio, Xiaokang Yang, and Junsong Yuan

More information about this series at http://www.springer.com/series/7899

Miguel Felix Mata-Rivera ·
Roberto Zagal-Flores · Javier Arellano Verdejo ·
Hugo Enrique Lazcano Hernandez (Eds.)

GIS LATAM

First Conference, GIS LATAM 2020
Mexico City, Mexico, September 28–30, 2020
Proceedings

 Springer

Editors
Miguel Felix Mata-Rivera ⓘ
Instituto Politécnico Nacional
México, Mexico

Roberto Zagal-Flores ⓘ
Instituto Politécnico Nacional
México, Mexico

Javier Arellano Verdejo ⓘ
El Colegio de la Frontera Sur
Chetumal, Mexico

Hugo Enrique Lazcano Hernandez ⓘ
El Colegio de la Frontera Sur
Chetumal, Mexico

ISSN 1865-0929 ISSN 1865-0937 (electronic)
Communications in Computer and Information Science
ISBN 978-3-030-59871-6 ISBN 978-3-030-59872-3 (eBook)
https://doi.org/10.1007/978-3-030-59872-3

This Springer imprint is published by the registered company Springer Nature Switzerland AG
The registered company address is: Gewerbestrasse 11, 6330 Cham, Switzerland

Preface

As this issue is being printed, the world is facing a lethal COVID-19 pandemic, with almost 22 million confirmed global cases. COVID-19 poses a tremendous challenge for leaders of nations who must strive to protect their communities across the globe. During these turbulent times, data-driven decisions have been made at both local and national levels to address alarming levels of COVID-19 cases. Hundreds of data analytics and visualizations have been created using spatial data, and the entire world has learned how to read GIS-based dashboards. By now, GIS applications have become some of the primary tools used by health and government officials, as well as the public, to get informed about the existing spatial COVID-19 risk on a local, regional, national, or global scale.

Meanwhile, global challenges have not ceased. We still need to find feasible solutions to critical issues affecting our communities and our world. GIS researchers play a significant role in helping advance understanding of earth processes and interconnected systems. The vision of GIS LATAM is to offer GIS researchers a platform to share significant findings that address these problems with the world.

First organized in 2019, the GIS LATAM conference was successfully attended at the venue and via live stream. GIS LATAM 2020 was organized as a virtual conference due to the pandemic, in order to provide an opportunity to advance dialogues concerning GIS education in higher education in Latin America and enable the presentation of the research featured in this issue. These proceedings include peer-reviewed research papers. Topics include COVID-19, biogas from waste, sargassum affecting Mexican coasts, and crime or pollution, to name a few. We are especially grateful to our colleagues whose first language is not English, who made an effort to offer their work in English to reach a wider audience. 29 research papers were submitted, including 2 invited papers. Three members of the conference Program Committee reviewed all submissions. 11 papers were accepted, yielding an acceptance rate of almost 40%.

The conference program included an interesting array of discussions and keynote lectures, with presentations of the research projects included in these proceedings. The reader may review the conference program in its entirety at www.gislatam.org.

The GIS LATAM Organizing Committee members want to express their gratitude to dozens of colleagues who devoted long hours to the research projects that are featured in this issue, as well as the reviewers of the submissions. We also want to thank those who helped organize the conference and made sure we included the most pressing topics and invited key researchers, educators, and practitioners. We especially extend our gratitude to ANTACOM A.C., Laboratory of Geospatial Intelligence and Mobile Computing of UPIITA-IPN, UPIITA staff members, and sponsors.

GIS LATAM 2020 was possible due to their selfless service and dedication to advance GIS in higher education in Latin America.

August 2020   Miriam Olivares

Organization

Organizing Committee

General Chair
Miguel Félix Mata-Rivera   UPIITA-IPN, Mexico

Regional Chairs
Javier Arellano Verdejo   El Colegio de la Frontera Sur, Mexico
Hugo Enrique Lazcano Hernandez   Cátedras CONACYT, El Colegio de la Frontera
                                   Sur, Mexico

International Co-chair
Miriam Olivares   Yale University, USA

Academic Chair
Roberto Zagal-Flores   ESCOM-IPN, Mexico

Local Manager
Jairo Zagal-Flores   UNADM, Mexico

Administrative Chair
Mauricio Zagal   ANTACOM A.C., Mexico

Program Committee

Christophe Claramunt   Naval Academy Research Institute, France
Andrea Ballatore   University of London, UK
Carlos Di Bella   INTA, Argentina
Manuel-Enrique Puebla-Martínez   UCI, Cuba
Diana Castro   ENCB-IPN, Mexico
Didier Leibovici   University of Nottingham, UK
Farid Karimipour   University of Tehran, Iran
Felipe O. Tapia Silva   UAM, Mexico
Gavin MacArdle   University College Dublin, Ireland
Georg Gartner   TU Vienna, Austria
Rosa Mercado   ESIME-ZAC, Mexico
Eduardo Loza   UNAM, Mexico
Zakaria Abdelmoiz Dahi   University of Constantine, Algeria
Hugo Barrera   UNAM, Mexico
Hugo Lazcano   Ecosur, Mexico

Javier Arellano	Ecosur, Mexico
Miriam Olivares	Yale University, USA
Cristian Barria	Universidad Mayor, Chile
Miguel Alonso	Universidad Mayor, Chile
Pedro Montes	Universidad Mayor, Chile
Hind Taud	CIDETEC-IPN, Mexico
Ki-Joune Li	Pusan University, South Korea
Kyoung-Sook Kim	AIST, Japan
María Elena Torres Olav	UACJ, Mexico
Mauro Gaio	LIUPPA, UPPA, France
Mohamed Sarwat	Arizona State University, USA
Roberto Zagal	ESCOM-IPN, Mexico
Sergio Ilarri	University of Zaragoza, Spain
Shoko Wakamiya	Kyoto Sangyo University, Japan
Willington Siabato	Universidad Nacional, Colombia
Xiang Li	East Normal China University, China
Cristian Barria	Universidad Mayor, Chile
Luis Manuel Gonzalez	Universidad Mayor, Chile
Clara Burbano	Colciencias, Colombia
Carolina Burbano	Colciencias, Colombia
Zakaria Abdelmoiz Dahi	University of Constantine, Algeria
Kamel Zeltni	University of Constantine, Algeria
Christian Cintrano	University of Malaga, Spain
Francisco Aragón	Universidad de Granada, Spain
Blanca Rico	UPIITA, Mexico
Jacobo G. Gonzalez Leon	UPIITA, Mexico

Sponsors

ANTACOM A.C.
UPIITA-IPN
GIS LATAM

Special Collaborators

FES ACATLAN-UNAM

Contents

Vulnerability Assessing Contagion Risk of Covid-19 Using Geographic Information Systems and Multi-Criteria Decision Analysis: Case Study Chetumal, México

Joan Alberto Sánchez-Sánchez[1](✉) ⓘ, Víctor Manuel Ku Chuc[2],
Efraín Alexander Ruíz Canché[3], and Francisco Javier Lara Uscanga[4]

[1] El Colegio de la Frontera Sur, Chetumal, Mexico
jasanchez@ecosur.mx
[2] Instituto Tecnológico de Chetumal, Chetumal, Mexico
[3] Comisión de Agua Potable y Alcantarillado del Estado de Q. Roo, Chetumal, Mexico
[4] Colegio Mexicano de Médicos Generales capítulo Chetumal, Chetumal,
Estado de México, Mexico

Abstract. The Covid-19 pandemic called SARS-CoV-2 and the declaration of a public health emergency of international importance aroused the interest of the scientific community in the assessment of risks and vulnerability related to viral infection. The purpose of this study was to evaluate and map the susceptibility of the risk to Covid-19 contagion in Chetumal, Mexico, by calibrating and applying a vulnerability model classified into four categories (extremely high, high, moderate and low) using Systems of Geographic Information (GIS) and Multi-Criteria Decision Analysis (MCDA). The objective refers to the achievement of a useful tool to help the health sector, local governments, the scientific community and the population in general to identify the best strategies to reduce contagion or restart local activities during quarantine conditions. For this purpose, a methodology based on GIS-MCDA was developed consisting of four stages and using nine essential criteria selected and evaluated by a transdisciplinary team of doctors and specialists in GIS. The vulnerability model made it possible to identify areas with extremely high vulnerability located towards the city center and in an area hosted by various service centers. Areas with high vulnerability defined in popular neighborhoods with high and medium degrees of marginalization. Areas with moderate vulnerability located around the areas of high vulnerability and areas of low vulnerability encompassing the perimeter areas of the city.

Keywords: Geographic Information Systems · Multi-Criteria Decision Analysis · Vulnerability assessing contagion risk of Covid-19

1 Introduction

By 30 January 2020, the world was shocked by the epidemic declaration of a new coronavirus called SARS-CoV-2 (Covid-19) as a public health emergency of international concern, causing severe acute respiratory syndrome (Grasselli et al. 2020). On 11

© Springer Nature Switzerland AG 2020
M. F. Mata-Rivera et al. (Eds.): GIS LATAM 2020, CCIS 1276, pp. 1–17, 2020.
https://doi.org/10.1007/978-3-030-59872-3_1

March 2020, the World Health Organization (WHO) declared the Covid-19 outbreak a pandemic due to the steady increase in number of cases outside China (WHO 2020). Covid-19 disease is highly contagious and the transmission can occur through direct contact by sucking droplets from secretions that an infected patient expels when coughing or sneezing, through indirect contact with surfaces in the immediate environment or with objects used by the infected person (Ong et al. 2020). Clinical symptoms of Covid-19 patients include fever, cough, fatigue and gastrointestinal infection (Guo et al. 2020). The elderly and people with underlying diseases are susceptible to infection and prone to serious outcomes (WHO 2020).

In Mexico, the first reported case of Covid-19 was on February 27 2020, through a person with history of having traveled to Italy causing a national alert, which initiated phase 1 of the epidemiological contingency (SSA 2020). On March 24 2020, the Mexican government instituted phase 2, called community contagion, establishing preventive and restrictive plans by applying the national day of healthy distance, suspension of mass events and concentrations of people in confined spaces, as well as the voluntary isolation of people. On April 21 2020, with the disease present throughout the country and 2,772 confirmed cases, phase 3 was announced as mandatory suspension of non-essential activities in public, private and social sectors (www.coronavirus.gob.mx). In this quarantine context, the entire country at this moment is experiencing a severe economic crisis with more than 12 million Mexicans without receiving economic income (SSA 2020).

The state of Quintana Roo, which is the world's leading national tourist destination and the eighth most popular tourist destination, reported on March 13 2020, its first case of Covid-19. Air, sea and land mobilization and migration movements with the countries of Belize and Guatemala were suspended and health surveillance became an element of strict order, guarantee and safety. Despite the most restrictive and temporary closing conditions, the number of infections has grown rapidly with an incidence rate of 339 cases per 100,000 inhabitants exceeding, the national average of 128 and compromising hospital occupation (Galera et al. 2020). This has led the local governments to adopt extraordinary, successful, and contingency plans by closing streets and avenues, and to apply the use of periphone, vehicle restriction and prohibition of the sale of alcoholic beverages without being able to stop the transmission chain. It is then imperative for the government and society to have methodologies to incorporate criteria, identified and weighted to support the local epidemiological surveillance system by improving decision-making to mitigate and control the spread of Covid-19.

Many researchers have established the use of MCDA and GIS as effective tools to identify and map areas of vulnerability and epidemic control (Qayum et al. 2015; Ahmad et al. 2017; Aboal-Viñas et al. 1999; Zemri and Hamdadou 2014; Honogh 2011). Vulnerability, is defined by Cardona (2003) as a community's economic, social or political predisposition to destabilization by an external phenomenon, natural or man-made, was defined in this study as the community's susceptibility to the risk of Covid-19 contagion. Among the different MCDA techniques, the most used is the Hierarchical Analytical Process (AHP) method developed by Saaty (1980). The basis of this proposal is that it allows numerical values to be assigned to the judgments made by individuals by allowing to quantify the contribution of each element of the hierarchy to the immediately higher level from which it is apparent (Berumen and Llamazares 2007). The AHP is very popular and widely used due to its easy understanding, interpretation and implementation of the results (Saaty 1978; 1979; 1980; Arulbalaji et al. 2019; Dar et al. 2020; Kaliraj et al. 2014; Kumar et al. 2018; 2020). The AHP uses paired comparisons by incorporating actor preferences between elements and uses a fundamental scale of 1, 3, 5, 7, 9 to incorporate judgments or assessments of the decision-making. This strictly positive scale allows to eliminate the ambiguities that human beings have when comparing elements in the proximity of zero or infinity (Moreno 2002). In addition, it allows to represent a wide range of decisions considering and combining qualitative and quantitative data, transforming a multidimensional problem (multicriterion) into a one-dimensional problem (scale of priorities) in which global outputs are represented (Assefa et al. 2018; Opricovic 2011; Saaty 2008).

On the other hand, the use of GIS tools applied to the health field is increasingly being used to examine the impact of distance, along with non-spatial factors to access and use health care services (Higgs 2004; 2009). According to National Center for Geographic Information and Analysis (1989) a GIS is an information system composed of hardware, software and procedures for capturing, handling, manipulating, analysing, modelling and representing georeferenced data, with the aim of solving management and planning and health problems (Aronoff 1989; Fernández et al. 2006). GIS is very useful for the study of the association between environment, location and health due to its ability to analyse and visualize data. They bring numerous advantages to practice for public health planning and research. They increase the possibility of identifying disease hotspots and linking them to social, cultural or environmental variables. They also identify high-risk groups by locating the most vulnerable spaces, as regards the social composition of the population (Suárez et al. 2020).

This work aims to evaluate and map the susceptibility of covid-19 risk to contagion in Chetumal, Mexico, by calibrating and applying a vulnerability model using Geographic Information Systems (GIS) and Multi-Decision Criteria Analysis (MCDA). The results of this study are expected to provide important scientific information for decision makers on the use of GIS tools to take pandemic prevention and control measures and serve as a reference for implementation in other cities or regions.

2 Study Area

The study area for this research was the City of Chetumal (Fig. 1), Capital State of Quintana Roo and municipality of Othón P. Blanco, whose name comes from Chactemal, which in Mayan language means place where red trees grow. It is located southeast of the Yucatan peninsula, at the geographic coordinates of 18° 30′ 13″ north latitude and 88° 18′ 19″ west longitude, covering an area of 42 km^2 (Hernández et al. 2014; Quivén 2016). Chetumal is the third most important city in the State with a population of 190,791 inhabitants and a growth rate above the national average (1.0%) (COESPO 2019). It borders the east with the Bay of Chetumal, to the south with the Río Hondo that marks the border with the country of Belize and to the west with the Bacalar lagoon system. The communication routes are to the north by federal highway No. 307 Chetumal to Cancún and to the west by federal highway No. 186 Chetumal to Escárcega (PDU 2018).

Most of its population extends north and east, locating itself in areas prone to floods and unsuitable for human settlement (Romero-Mayo 2012). Economic activities belong to the services, tourism, government administration, and self-consumption agriculture sectors (Fragoso-Servón and Pereira 2018).

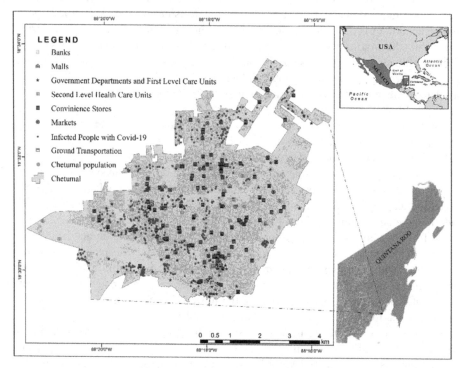

Fig. 1. Location map of the study area

The climate is warm sub-humid with rains in summer (INEGI 2009). The average temperature is 26 °C, the warmest month is in July and the warmest in December. The average annual precipitation is 1,300 mm and the highest precipitation is in summer. The study area is hurricane prone. The gleysol-type soil predominates, characterized by poor drainage, with vegetation cover of the upper jungle and medium sub-evergreen (INEGI 2016). Physiographically, the city is characterized by descending stepped reliefs from west to east with little elevation above sea level (Quivén 2016). The upper part of the city reaches nine mamsl and the lower zone two mamsl. Limestone is found superficially, traditionally known as flagstone. The water flow is underground and the water table is shallow. The geology of the city is made up of Tertiary and Quaternary sedimentary rocks, both periods of the Cenozoic Era (Sánchez Crispín 1980).

3 Methodology

In this study, GIS-based techniques and the MCDA methodology (GIS-MCDA) were used to assess and map the susceptibility of the risk to Covid-19 contagion by calibrating and applying a vulnerability model (Fig. 2). The calculation of the GIS-MCDA was developed considering four main stages: 1) definition of the problem and selection of essential criteria, 2) acquisition of data and spatial analysis in GIS, 3) MCDA through the AHP technique and calculation of the ratio of consistency, 4) MCDA-GIS procedure.

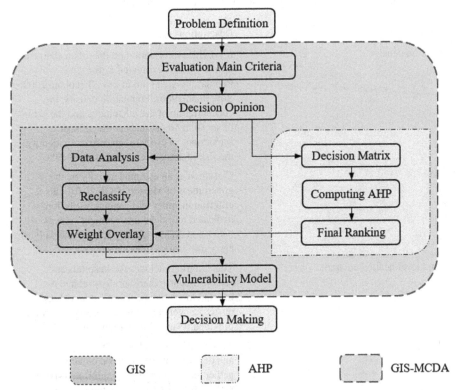

Fig. 2. Geographic Information System and Multi-Criteria Decision Analysis (GIS-MCDA) developed in this study using the Analytical Hierarchy Process (AHP) technique.

3.1 Definition of the Problem and Selection of Essential Criteria

The first stage consisted of analyzing the risk of Covid-19 contagion in urban establishments and public places to determine the elements involved and classify them into essential criteria. The problem was structured using the Analytical Hierarchy Process (AHP) technique described by Saaty (2008). To calculate the Covid-19 contagion risk vulnerability index, the variable with the greatest weight or value within each dimension obtained according to the AHP method was selected.

According to the multi-criteria approach and with the participation of a transdisciplinary team of doctors and GIS specialists, nine essential criteria were selected. This includes population density, distance to banks, distance to second-level health care units, distance to shopping malls, distance to convenience stores, distance to markets, distance to government agencies and first-level care units, distance to terminals and distance to infected people with Covid-19. The description and justification of each criterion is presented in Table 1.

Table 1. Description and justification of the criteria used in the AHP.

Criteria	Description
Population density	It provides information on the urban character of a city and is expressed as the Population/Area ratio in km^2 (Escolano 2002; Silverman 1986). Population density, the concentration of the inhabitants and the habits of social aggregation become of basic importance in every urban district to identify the risk of contagion (Sohrabi et al. 1986)
Banks	Classified as an essential activity by the government of Mexico (DOF 2020), this criterion includes all financial institutions dedicated to money management such as banks and ATMs, where people come daily to carry out various transactions
Second level health care units	This criterion includes the hospitals and establishments where services related to internal medicine, pediatrics, gynecology, obstetrics, general surgery and psychiatry are provided (García 2006; Etchebarne 2001)
Malls	This criterion includes all shopping centers and department stores whose objective is to gather, in closed and air-conditioned spaces, various proposals so that potential customers can make their purchases more comfortably. They also serve as recreational sites, where the highest concentration of people occurs mainly on weekends and evening hours.
Convenience stores	This criterion includes self-service stores with less than 500 m^2 (Kuo et al. 2002), most of these stores are practically identical in essence and are open 24 h a day, seven days a week. Food, personal and household hygiene products, pre-paid cards and ATMs are some of the services offered by these points of sale and are strategically located in places with a higher population densit

(continued)

Table 1. (*continued*)

Criteria	Description
Public markets	The public market criterion was defined as the traditional type food supply shops characterized by the formation of various stages of intermediation between production regions and consumption spaces, with multiple channels in retail distribution such as stalls or miscellaneous (Torres 2011). These shops, concentrating a large population at certain times, are popular for selling fruits, vegetables, meats, poultry and seafood, in addition to having a restaurant area. Globally, diseases caused by food consumption in public markets have been widely reported (Muñoz et al. 2011; Franco et al. 2013; Zhu et al. 2020)
Government agencies and first-level care units	Government agencies included all institutions dedicated to public administration and management at the federal, state, and municipal levels, administered and financed by the Mexican government (INEGI 2014). The First Level Care Units include the spaces that provide outpatient care for the most frequent morbidity and are dedicated to health care, prevention and promotion and are recognized by the population as local health benchmarks (Martín and Cano 1999)
Terminals	Includes ground transportation services with facilities and equipment for boarding and disembarking passengers and/or cargo. The East Bus Terminal (ADO) and the foreign taxi service of the Single Union of Rental Car Drivers (SUCHAA) were the main sites selected for this criterion

(*continued*)

Table 1. (*continued*)

Criteria	Description
Infected people with Covid-19	This criterion includes the geographic location of patients with Covid-19 disease at home. Many people who contract the SARS COV-2 virus do not require hospitalization, they are only monitored by doctors who control the disease and the daily status of its evolution. Although the infected patient remains at home, inadequate waste management and lack of cleaning and sanitation can increase the risk of contagion among neighbors. The data incorporated into the GIS-MCDA are those reported by the Secretary of Health of the state of Quintana Roo at the cut of June 18, 2020 with a total of 414 positive cases

3.2 Data Acquisition and Spatial Analysis in GIS

The second stage consisted in (1) the acquisition of spatial information on Chetumal's demographic, pandemic and infrastructure aspects and 2) the use of spatial analysis tools (kernel density, Euclidean distance, and reclassification) for the later stage of the MCDA-GIS procedure.

For the acquisition of information, each establishment was located using a Magellan Mobile Mapper 6 brand Global Positioning System (GPS) using the Universal Transverse Mercator (UTM zone 16 N) coordinate system. In addition, estimated population data in 2020 of Chetumal were obtained from the Facebook Connectivity Laboratory and Center for the International Earth Science Information Network (CIESIN 2016). The kernel density tool was used only to calculate the population density criterion. Conceptually, the goal of kernel density estimation is to calculate the density of points in a given area using the distance between the points, if and only if, the points have the same weight (Roig-Tierno et al. 2013). The search radius was 564.19 m (1 km^2 area). Subsequently, the kernel density was classified into five categories using the reclassification tool, with 1 being the category with the lowest population density and 5 being the highest population density (Fig. 3a).

For the remaining eight criteria, the Euclidean distance tool was used to describe the relationship of each cell to a set of origins based on the distance of the straight line (ESRI 2019). Among the functionalities of the Euclidean distance algorithm, its usefulness for determining the similarity between two things or pairs of data stands out. It is calculated from the center of the source cell to the center of each of the surrounding cells. Conceptually, it works as follows: for each cell, the distance to each source cell is determined by calculating the hypotenuse with X_max and Y_max. Subsequently, each criterion was reclassified into five categories using proximity distances to represent the risk vulnerability to Covid-19 contagion; five being the nearest distance and one the furthest distance (Table 2).

3.3 MCDA Through the AHP Technique and Calculation of the Consistency Ratio

The third stage used the AHP method developed by Saaty (1980; 2000; 2008) to assign the weights of importance to each criterion. In this method weights can be derived by taking the priority vector of a square reciprocal matrix of pairwise comparisons between criteria; comparisons deal with the relative importance of the two criteria involved. The scores in the comparison matrix were assigned on a continuous scale of 1 to 9, also considering the reciprocals of those scores (Table 2). Score 1 represented equal importance, 3 moderate importance, 5 strong importance, 7 very strong importance and 9 absolute importance. The consistency ratio (CR), which measures the inconsistency level of the pairwise comparison matrix (i.e. the probability that the factor weights were randomized), was calculated using the mathematical ratio

$$CR = CI/RI \tag{1}$$

Where CR is the consistency ratio; CI Consistency Index; RI Random Index, which indicates the consistency of a random matrix.

$$CI = (\lambda_{max} - n)/(n - 1) \tag{2}$$

CI Consistency Index; λ max is the maximum eigenvalue; n the dimension of the decision matrix.

Table 2. Rankin and weights of the criteria used in Weighted Overlay

Ranking	Criteria	Proximity distances	Percentage (%)
1	Second level health care units	<100, 100–200, 200–250, 250–300, >300	31
2	Markets	<75, 75–150, 150--00, 200–250, >250	20
3	Infected people with Covid-19	<50, 50–75, 75–100, 100–200, >200	18
4	Banks	<25, 25–50, 50–75, 75–100, >100	9
5	Malls	<75, 75–150, 150–200, 200–250, >250	7
6	Government departments and first level care units	<75, 75–150, 150–200, 200–250, >250	6
7	Ground transportation	<25, 25–50, 50–75, 75–100, >100	5
8	Conviniencie stores	<25, 25–50, 50–75, 75–100, >100	2
9	Population density	<2680, 2681–5360, 5361–8050, 8051–10730, 10731–13450	2

The CR must have a value less than 0.1 (<10%) to indicate that the method is acceptable (Saaty 1980). The consistency ratio in this study was 0.06 (6%), being below the maximum consistency ratio recommended by Saaty.

3.4 MCDA-GIS Procedure

In the fourth stage, the Weighted Overlay tool was used to generate the vulnerability map model using the weights obtained from the calculation of the priority vector within the AHP. The value of the vulnerability model was classified into four categories: low vulnerability (value 1), moderate vulnerability (value 2), high vulnerability (value 3) and extremely high vulnerability (value 4).

The GIS through the ArcMap 10.7 ESRI (2019) software, were used as a tool for the development of this study. The maps were worked in raster format with a spatial resolution of 2 meters, allowing greater efficiency in the structure for overlapping maps.

4 Results and Discussions

Describing the first and second stages of the procedure, we achieve the geographic location and quantification of 699 establishments corresponding to eight essential criteria without considering the population density criterion. This includes 13 banks, 29 second-level health care units, 13 shopping centers, 121 convenience stores, 7 markets, 64 government agencies and first-level care units, 7 terminals and 414 infected people with Covid-19. The influence of the criteria involved in the propagation of the Covid-19 was quantified by reclassifying the essential criteria calculated with the kernel density and Euclidean distance into five categories using the ARCGIS 10.8 program.

Generally, urban density is defined by the building-to-land ratio or the floor area ratio (SAR et al. 2015). However, they are basically estimated through the use of data from cartographic servers that are not always available and are expensive. Therefore, in the present study, we have used the data from CIESIN (2016) with the help of GIS to map the population density or human settlements of Chetumal. According to Fig. 3a in the study area it is observed that the population density is high in the central north and west areas. The north central part is made up of popular colonies inhabited by people with a medium degree of marginalization, a relatively low socioeconomic level and workers employed in the informal sector (COESPO 2010). The western part with a high degree of marginalization was mostly characterized by irregular human settlements which are, in some cases, the only option for families in poverty to access land to build their homes. Population density is one of the most important indices because it not only indicates the construction density but also indirectly the daytime population corresponding to economic power. The raster layer resulting from the reclassification was integrated in stage four of this study.

Figure 3 a–i, illustrate the reclassification procedure using the results of the kernel density and Euclidean distance. In accordance with an exhaustive discussion by the transdisciplinary team and the support of Mexican Official Standards, 5 areas of influence were defined in each criterion, ranging from 0 to the maximum value, to establish restrictions on the risk of Covid-19 contagion. These restrictions were established by colors according to their magnitude of risk, with red being the most dangerous area and blue being the least risky area.

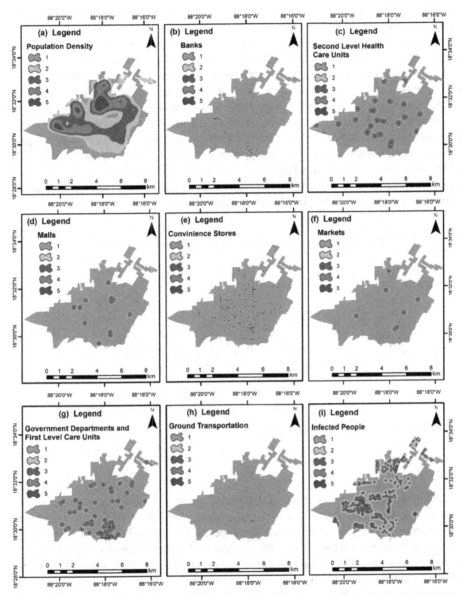

Fig. 3. Reclassified Map with Euclidean distance and kernel density **a** Population density **b** Banks **c** Second Level Health Care Units **d** Malls **e** Convenience Stores **f** Markets **g** Government Departments and First Level Care Units **h** Ground transportation **g** Infected people (Color figure online)

In addition, with the results of the GIS-MCDA procedure, we have performed a weighted overlay operation through the ArcGIS spatial analysis tool to obtain the areas of vulnerability to the risk of contagion of Covid-19 from Chetumal. In particular, nine weights were defined and calibrated using the multicriteria approach through the AHP technique (Table 3). The resulting influence was expressed as a percentage and the description of the results follows the classification parameters proposed in the first stage. Second Level Health Care Units (31%) including public and private hospitals and health centers was the most important criterion because they are the establishments most exposed to contagion due to the type of service they offer during the 24 h. In addition to the patient seeking late help, he comes when his symptoms are shortness of breath and oxygen, giving a possible case of Covid-19. This condition makes it more risky and increases the probability of being transmitted horizontally, to the point of causing saturation in hospital services, causing them to collapse due to the number of people seeking care without need, in addition to the relatives of hospitalized patients who are heavily exposed to contagion when meeting in the emergency and hospitalization areas without respecting prevention and hygiene protocols.

Table 3. Pairwise comparison matrix for assessing the weights

Criteria	1	2	3	4	5	6	7	8	9
1	1	1/5	1	5	1/5	7	3	3	1/3
2	5	1	5	9	3	9	5	5	3
3	1	1/5	1	3	1/3	5	1	3	1/3
4	1/5	1/9	1/3	1	1/7	1	1/5	1/3	1/7
5	5	1/3	3	7	1	7	5	7	1
6	1/7	1/9	1/5	1	1/7	1	1/5	1/5	1/7
7	1/3	1/5	1	5	1/5	5	1	1	1/5
8	1/3	1/5	1/3	3	1/7	5	1	1	1/7
9	3	1/3	3	7	1	7	5	7	1

Public markets (20%) were the second strongest criterion due to the strong concentration of people who visit them to do their shopping, in addition to the small spaces that exist in them. The third strongest criterion was people infected with Covid-19 (18%) due to the ability to transmit the virus to other people such as family and friends who do not respect prevention and hygiene measures. The criteria Banks (9%), Malls (7%), Government Departments and First Level Care Units (6%), Ground Transportation (5%), Convenience Stores (2%) and Population Density (2%) were the criteria with lower weight (weight) of importance without discredit its value in the general analysis.

Criteria 1 Banks 2 s Level Health Care Units 3 Malls 4 Conveniencie Stores 5 Markets 6 Population Density 7 Government Departments and First Level Care Units 8 Ground Transportation 9 Infected people with Covid-19. $\lambda_{max} = 9.75$, CI $= 0.09$, RI $= 1.45$ (Saaty, 2008) CR $= 0.06 < 0.1$ (consistency is acceptable).

4.1 Covid-19 Contagion Risk Vulnerability

To show the potential of the model, the proposed GIS-MCDA approach was used to obtain four areas of Covid-19 contagion risk vulnerability as depicted in Fig. 4. The extremely high vulnerability category represented 0.03%, the high vulnerability category 2.55%, moderate vulnerability 26.75% and low vulnerability 70.68%. The model allowed defining two areas with extremely high vulnerability, the first, located in the city center at the intersections of Benito Juárez and Efraín Aguilar avenues, where establishments for public use are located such as the Museum of the city of Chetumal, hospital Morelos, Potable Water Commission of Quintana Roo and the private university UNID, and a second, at the intersections of Avenue San Salvador and Calle Agustín Olachea, where the Campestre and Montecristo clinics, Banorte and HSBC banks, Super Akí self-service store, are located. Oxxo convenience store, and the integral friendship park. Both areas are characterized by high vehicle-pedestrian traffic. The areas with high vulnerability are delimited in the Central colonies, Italia, Guadalupe Victoria, Solidaridad, Proterritorio, Sian Kaan I and II, Fovissste II, Payo Obispo and Pacto Obrero. It is easily foreseeable that all of them encompass most of the geolocated establishments in stage two of this study. The zone of moderate vulnerability is located around the areas of high vulnerability, however, due to the conditions of the criteria, it is possible to observe large areas scattered throughout the city, covering different urban sectors.

Finally, the areas of low vulnerability presented a more stable pattern within the city and despite having the highest percentage of surface, the fact of not being close to or immersed in points of high confluence mean that these areas are not risky and can be passable by applying prevention measures and security established by local governments. The results obtained suggest for local administrators to define specific useful strategies to safeguard low risk and keep the economy active at the same time.

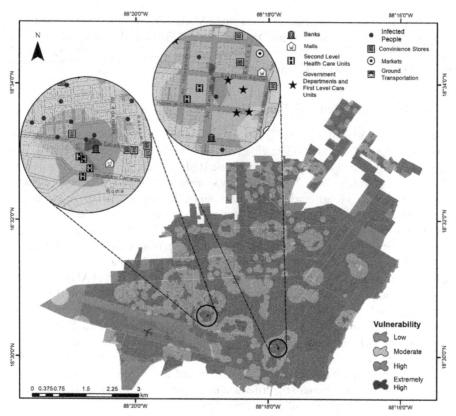

Fig. 4. Contagion risk vulnerability map for Covid-19 in Chetumal.

5   Conclusion

The present study was related to the determination of the vulnerability and the risk of contagion of Covid-19 in the City of Chetumal by using a multi-criteria approach using AHP and GIS techniques. The use of AHP allowed reducing the subjectivity of the evaluation criteria by evaluating each of the criteria independently. GIS integrated with the multi-criteria approach are shown as a simple and powerful tool for decision-making regarding pandemic prevention and control.

The vulnerability model allowed to identify two areas with extremely high vulnerability (0.03%), located in the city center and in an area collected by various services. The areas with high vulnerability (2.55%) were delimited mainly in popular colonies with high and medium degrees of marginalization, the areas of moderate vulnerability (26.75%) were located around the areas of high vulnerability and without a defined pattern and the areas of low vulnerability (70.68%) presented a more stable pattern in the perimeter areas of the city.

Health officials, heads of local governments, the scientific community and the general population can easily use the results of this study while the Health Emergency in our country continues. Furthermore, under the MCDA-GIS approach proposed in this study, the data can be easily updated and published using interactive maps and web tools available now. Identifying the geographical areas with the highest vulnerability to contagion will allow the implementation of more rigorous measures in those places where the greatest number of people are concentrated, minimizing the incidence and mortality rates related to this disease.

References

Aboal Viñas, J.L., et al.: El procedimiento de toma de decisión para controlar la epidemia de meningitis C en Galicia en 1996. Gac. Sanit. **13**, 62–69 (1999)

Ahmad, F., Goparaju, L., Qayum, A.: Studying malaria epidemic for vulnerability zones: multicriteria approach of geospatial tools. J. Geosci. Environ. Prot. **5**(5), 30–53 (2017)

Aronoff, S.: Geographic Information Systems: A Management Perspective. WDL Publications, Ottawa (1989)

Arulbalaji, P., Padmalal, D., Sreelash, K.: GIS and AHP techniques based delineation of groundwater potential zones: a case study from Southern Western Ghats, India. Sci. Rep. **9**, 1–17 (2019)

Assefa, T., Jha, M., Reyes, M., Srinivasan, R., Worqlul, A.W.: Assessment of suitable areas for home gardens for irrigation potential, water availability, and water-lifting technologies. Water **10**(4), 495 (2018)

Berumen, S.A., Llamazares, F.: La utilidad de los métodos de decisión multicriterio (como el AHP) en un entorno de competitividad creciente [The utility of multi-criteria decision methods (such as AHP) in an increasingly competitive environment]. Cuadernos Administrativos Bogotá (Colombia) **20**(34), 65–87 (2007)

Cardona, O.D.: The need for rethinking the concepts of vulnerability and risk from a holistic perspective: a necessary review and criticism of effective risk assessment. In: Bankoff, G., Frerks, D., Hillhorst, D. (eds.) Mapping Vulnerability: Disasters, Development and People. Earthscan Publishers, London (2003)

CIESIN. Center for International Earth Science Information Network: High Resolution Settlement Layer (HRSL). Columbia University (2016)

COESPO. http://coespo.qroo.gob.mx/Descargas/doc/PUBLICACCIONES%20DE%20INTE RES/POBLACION_QROO_2019.pdf. Accessed 02 Jul 2020

Dar, T., Rai, N., Bhat, A.: Delineation of potential groundwater recharge zones using analytical hierarchy process (AHP). Geol. Ecol. Landscapes **00**, 1–16 (2020)

DOF. Diario Oficial de la Federación: Acuerdo por el que se establecen acciones extraordinarias para atender la emergencia sanitaria generada por el virus SARS-CoV2. México (2020)

Escolano, S.: Densidad de población y sustentabilidad en la ciudad de Zaragoza. In: Longares Alardeen, L.A., Pek Monné, J.L. (eds.) Aportaciones geográficas en memoria del projesor L. Miguel Yetano Ruiz. Zaragoza. Departa ~ nento de Geografía y Ordenación del Territorio. Universidad de Zaragoza, pp. 173–182 (2002)

ESRI A: ArcGIS 10.8. Environmental Systems Research Institute, Redlands, CA (2019)

Etchebarne, L.: Atención Primaria de la Salud y Primer Nivel de Atención. In: Etchebarne, L. (ed.) Temas de Medicina Preventiva y Social, pp. 75–82. Montevideo, Fefmur (2001)

Fernández-Núñez, H.M.: SIG-ESAC: sistema de información geográfica para la gestión de la estadística de salud de Cuba. Rev. Cubana Hig. Epidemiol. **44**(3) (2006)

Fragoso-Servón, P., Pereira, A.: Suelos y Karst, origen de inundaciones y hundimientos en Chetumal, Quintana Roo, México. In: European Scientific Journal, no. 14, ESJ (2018)

Franco, P., Ramírez, L., Orozco, M., López, L.: Determinación de Escherichia coli e identificación del serotipo O157:H7 en carne de cerdo comercializada en los principales supermercados de la ciudad de Cartagena. Rev. Lasallista Invest. **10**(1), 91–100 (2013)

Galera, A.: Chetumal es líder nacional por casos activos de Covid-19. Novedades, pp. 1–3 (2020)

García, J.: Sobrevivirán los niveles de atención a la revolución de la salud publica cubana. Rev. Cubana Salud Pública **32**(1), 07–15 (2006)

Grasselli, G., Zangrillo, A., Zanella, A., et al.: Baseline characteristics and outcomes of 1591 patients infected with SARS-CoV-2 admitted to ICUs of the lombardy region. JAMA **323**(323), 1574–1581 (2020)

Guo, Y., Cao, Q., Hong, Z., et al.: The origin, transmission and clinical therapies on coronavirus disease 2019 (COVID-19) outbreak – an update on the status. Mil. Med. Res. **7**, 11 (2020)

Hernández, M.: Evaluación del riesgo y vulnerabilidad ante la amenaza de huracanes en zonas costeras del Caribe Mexicano: Chetumal y Mahahual. Universidad de Quintana Roo. Tesis de doctorado, p. 161 (2014)

Higgs, G.: A literature review of the use of GIS-based measures of access to health care services. Health Serv. Outcomes Res. Methodol. **5**(2), 119–139 (2004)

Higgs, G.: The role of GIS for health utilization studies: literature review. Health Serv. Outcomes Res. Method. **9**, 84–99 (2009)

Honogh, V., et al.: Spatially explicit multi-criteria decision analysis for managing vector-borne diseases. Int. J. Health Geogr. **10**, 70 (2011)

INEGI. Instituto Nacional de Estadística, Geografía e Informática: Prontuario de información geográfica municipal de los Estados Unidos Mexicanos Othón P. Blanco, Quintana Roo. México, D.F. (2009)

INEGI. Instituto Nacional de Estadística, Geografía e Informática: Catálogo de Dependencias e Instituciones de Interés Público, México (2014)

INEGI. Instituto Nacional de Estadística, Geografía e Informática: Anuario estadístico y geográfico de Quintana Roo. México (2016)

Kaliraj, S., Chandrasekar, N., Magesh, N.S.: Identification of potential groundwater recharge zones in vaigai upper basin, Tamil Nadu, using GIS-based analytical hierarchical process (AHP) technique. Arab. J. Geosci. **7**, 1385–1401 (2014)

Kumar, A., Mondal, N.C., Ahmed, S.: Identification of groundwater potential zones using RS, GIS and AHP techniques: a case study in a part of Deccan Volcanic Province (DVP), Maharashtra, India. J. Indian Soc. Remote Sens. **48**, 497–511 (2020)

Kumar, A., Krishna, A.P.: Assessment of groundwater potential zones in coal mining impacted hard-rock terrain of India by integrating geospatial and analytic hierarchy process (AHP) approach. Geocarto Int. **33**, 105–129 (2018)

Kuo, R., Chi, S., Kao, S.: A decision support system for selecting convenience store location through integration of fuzzy AHP and artificial neural network. Comput. Ind. **47**, 199–214 (2002)

Martín, A., Cano, J.: Compendio De Atención Primaria. Editorial Harcourt, San Diego (1999)

Moreno-Jiménez, J.M.: El proceso analítico jerárquico. fundamentos. metodología y aplicaciones. In: Caballero, R., Fernández, G.M. (eds.) Toma de decisiones con criterios múltiples. RECT@. Revista Electrónica de Comunicaciones y Trabajos de ASEPUMA. Serie Monografías, vol. 1, pp. 21–53 (2002)

Muñoz, A., Vargas, M., Otero, L., Díaz, G., Guzmán, V.: Presencia de Listeria monocytogenes en alimentos listos para el consumo, procedentes de plazas de mercado y delicatessen de supermercados de cadena, Bogotá, D.C., 2002–2008. Biomédica **31**(3), 428–439 (2011)

NCGIA. National Center for Geographic Information and Analysis: El plan de investigación del Centro Nacional de Información y Análisis Geográfico. Revista Internacional de Sistemas de Información Geográfica **3**(2), 117–36 (1989)

Ong, S.W., et al.: Air, surface environmental, and personal protective equipment contamination by severe acute respiratory syndrome coronavirus 2 (SARS-CoV-2) from a symptomatic patient. JAMA **323**(16), 1610–1612 (2020)

Opricovic, S.: Fuzzy VIKOR with an application to water resources planning. Expert Syst. Appl. **38**, 12983–12990 (2011)

PDU: Programa de Desarrollo Urbano de Chetumal-Calderitas-Subteniente López-Huay-Pix y Xul-Há. Municipio de Othón P. Blanco, Estado de Quintana Roo (2018)

Qayum, A., Arya, R., Kumar, P. Lynn, A.M.: Socio-economic, epidemiological and geographic features based GIS-integrated mapping to identify malarial hotspot. Malaria J. **14**, 192 (2015)

Quivén, J.: Propuesta de vivienda social sostenible para climas cálidos. Aplicación en la ciudad de Chetumal, Q.R., México. Universitat Politécnica de Catalunya. Master en Ingeniería de la Edificación. p. 51 (2016)

Roig-Tierno, N., Baviera-Puig, A., Buitrago-Vera, J.: Business opportunities analysis using GIS: the retail distribution sector. Global Bus. Perspect. **1**(3), 226–238 (2013)

Romero-Mayo, R.: Chetumal: problemática urbana en una ciudad media en la costa sur del Caribe mexicano. Perspectiva Geográfica **17**, 147–168 (2012)

Saaty, T.L.: Modeling unstructured decision problems the theory of analytical hierarchies. Math. Comput. Simul. **20**(3), 147–158 (1978)

Saaty, T.L.: Applications of analytical hierarchies. Math. Comput. Simul. **21**(1), 1–20 (1979)

Saaty, T.L.: The Analytic Network Process (ANP). RWS Publications, Pittsburgh (1980)

Saaty, T.L.: The Fundamentals of Decision-Making and Priority Theory with the Analytic Hierarchy Process. RWS Publications, Pitsburg (2000)

Saaty, T.L.: Decision making with the analytic hierarchy process. Int. J. Serv. Sci. **1**(1), 83–98 (2008)

Sánchez Crispín, A.: Características generales del medio físico de Quintana Roo. Memorias del Simposio: Quintana Roo: Problemática y perspectiva, México, UNAM. Instituto de Geología, CIQRO, pp. 29–36 (1980)

Sar, N., Chatterjee, S., Das Adhikari, M.: Integrated remote sensing and GIS based spatial modelling through analytical hierarchy process (AHP) for water logging hazard, vulnerability and risk assessment in Keleghai river basin, India. Model. Earth Syst. Environ. **1**, 31 (2015)

Silverman, B.W.: Estimación de densidad para las estadísticas y el análisis de datos. Chapman and Hall, New York (1986)

SSA. Secretaría de Salud de México: Informe Financiero de la Secretaría de Salud por COVID-19, México (2020)

Sohrabi, C., et al.: World Health Organization declares global emergency: a review of the 2019 novel coronavirus (COVID-19). Int. J. Surg. **76**, 71–76 (2020)

Suárez, L., et al.: Índice de vulnerabilidad ante el COVID-19 en Mexico. In: Investigaciones Geográficas, pp. 2448–7279 (2020)

Torres-Torres, F.: El abasto de alimentos en México hacia una transición económica y territorial. Problemas Del Desarrollo. Revista Latinoamericana De Econom **42**(166), 63–84 (2011)

WHO Director-General's opening remarks at the media briefing on COVID-19, 11 March (2020) https://www.who.int/dg/speeches/detail/who-director-general-s-opening-remarks-at-the-media-briefing-on-covid-19—11-march-2020. Accessed 20 Mar 2020

Zemri, F., Hamdadou, D.: Integration of multi criteria analysis methods to a spatio temporal decision support system for epidemiological monitoring. In: ICAASE 2014, pp. 116–123 (2014)

Zhu, N., Zhang, D., Wang, W., et al.: A novel coronavirus from patients with pneumonia in China, 2019. N. Engl. J. Med. **382**, 727–733 (2020)

Land Subsidence in Villahermosa Tabasco Mexico, Using Radar Interferometry

Zenia Pérez-Falls⬛ and Guillermo Martínez-Flores$^{(⊠)}$⬛

Instituto Politécnico Nacional, Centro Interdisciplinario de Ciencias Marinas, Av. Instituto Politécnico Nacional S/N, Col. Playa Palo de Santa Rita, 23096 La Paz, B.C.S, México
zperezf1600@alumno.ipn.mx, gmflores@ipn.mx

Abstract. Land subsidence is a geological phenomenon that consists of the gradual sinking of the earth's crust and can damage to the urban infrastructure and the population. This phenomenon is caused, among other factors, by the overexploitation of aquifers and the excessive extraction of hydrocarbons. The Synthetic Aperture Differential Radar Interferometry (DInSAR) technique has been used since the late 1990s to detect deformations on the ground, including subsidence in higher spatial and temporal coverage compared to traditional methods such as geodesic, instrumental, GPS at a sensitivity of mm/year. The Villahermosa city, Tabasco, concentrates 512 oil wells in an area of 10 km^2 located in the northwest of the town. The DInSAR technique was implemented to quantify the subsidence of the land in the Villahermosa city. Twenty-eight SAR images from the Sentinel-1A satellite from 2014 to 2018 were used. These images were processed with SNAP, the SNAPHU algorithm, and QGIS. Maximum land subsidence of 4 cm/year (2014–2015) was obtained in the southwest region in an area of 327 ha. For the period 2016–2018, the land subsidence was 15 cm/year in an extension of 6,232 ha.

Keywords: DInSAR · Sentinel-1A · SAR · Urban nucleus

1 Introduction

Subsidence is considered a risk factor in urban areas. Subsidence is a type of land collapse characterized by near-vertical deformation or settlement of earth materials [1]. The study of subsidence in urban areas is essential, where the damages caused can become considerable, being a significant risk for the urban infrastructure [2].

Surfaces that can be affected by subsidence can occupy areas from a few square meters to thousands of square kilometers [3].

Land subsidence has been calculated using traditional geodetic techniques such as leveling, Global Positioning Implementation Systems (GPS), as well as instrumental methods. Also, methodologies have been implemented with synthetic aperture radars (SAR), such as interferometry (InSAR) and differential interferometry (DInSAR), which began to be developed from the 1990s.

Many investigations have been carried out to obtain the deformation of the terrain associated with various causes such as water extraction [4, 5], mining exploitation [6, 7],

© Springer Nature Switzerland AG 2020
M. F. Mata-Rivera et al. (Eds.): GIS LATAM 2020, CCIS 1276, pp. 18–29, 2020.
https://doi.org/10.1007/978-3-030-59872-3_2

geothermal fields [8, 9], river delta [10, 11], anthropic influence [12, 13], hydrocarbon extraction [14, 15], among others.

This last technique has become a useful and essential tool in remote sensing as it can estimate both spatial and temporal surface movements due to ground subsidence [16]. DInSAR has a series of advantages compared to traditional geodetic and instrumental techniques, such as its wide spatial coverage in different areas, such as urban areas, and being able to be used as monitoring services at lower costs [2]. The possibility of the DInSAR technique to detect subsidence makes it viable to monitor almost any earth structure subject to displacement [17].

1.1 SAR Images and DInSAR

SAR images are used to implement a conventional technique in which the terrain is illuminated with electromagnetic waves of microwave frequency [9, 17]. The wave round-trip time and the signal amplitude reflected by objects in the ground are used to determine the distances from the sensor to the ground and generate a two-dimensional image of the interest area [18]. The bright regions in a radar image represent a large amplitude of the returned wave energy, which depends on the surface slope and the roughness and dielectric characteristics of the surface material [18]. Amplitude is a measure of the target's reflectivity, while the phase encodes changes in the surface, and a term proportional to the range of the target [17, 18].

The InSAR technique began to be implemented in the late 1990s. It consists of exploiting the information contained in the phase of at least two SAR images taken from slightly different points in the same area. The images are processed to relate the difference between their distances to the same point on the ground with the scene topography [9, 19]. InSAR uses the phase information in two SAR images to determine the phase difference between each pair of points in the corresponding images, thus producing an interferogram.

Differential SAR interferometry (DInSAR) is a variant of InSAR. It is an image processing technique that allows the generation of terrain displacement maps and the calculation of relative coherence [20]. It is also used to detect and measure movements so small that the topography component must be discarded [17].

The primary sources of noise and error of the InSAR technique are the loss of coherence due to the high intensity of the vegetation, the lack of temporal correlation, the topographic residuals due to the precision of the Digital Elevation Model (DEM) and the atmospheric factors such as temperature and variations of water vapor in the atmosphere [21].

2 Study Area

The study area corresponds to Villahermosa city in the Centro municipality, Tabasco, with an area of 61,232 ha. The Villahermosa city, the capital of Tabasco, is in the Southeast region of the country at 92° 55′ west longitude and 17° 59′ north latitude, corresponding to the physiographic region of the Southern Gulf Coastal Plain sub-province Tabasco Plains and Swamps [23] (see Fig. 1).

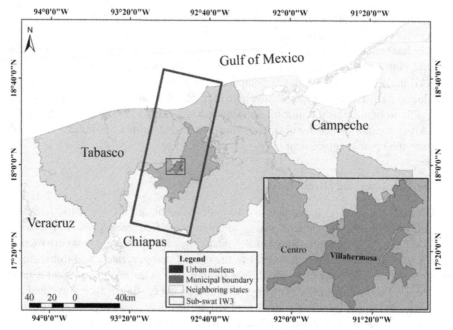

Fig. 1. Study area location. The red rectangle shows the sub-swath IW3, corresponding to the scene of a Sentinel-1A satellite image with descending orbit. (Color figure online)

This city is in the floodplain of the Grijalva River, being the most important urban settlement in Tabasco, due to the development in recent decades of hydrocarbon extraction as the main economic activity [23]. The oil boom in the 1960s was a determining factor for urban growth, beginning in the second half of the 20th century, as it became the main economic activity. This boom led to an increase from 23,947 (first half of the 20th century) to 297,268 inhabitants [23, 24].

Regarding lithology, it is based on sandstone and sedimentary rocks from the Cenozoic era [25]. A predominance of soils formed in the alluvial quaternary is found. The most abundant soils are gleysols characterized by a clay texture, and slow drainage, formed on unconsolidated materials.

The area belongs to the Hydrological Region Grijalva-Usumacinta, the largest and most flowing region in Mexico. It has a wide lake system with a high density of bodies of water. Hydrological conditions contribute to the area being subject to flooding [22] due to the high precipitation regime. The topography characterizes the area with few slopes, as well as the low permeability of the soils [22, 23]. Furthermore, in the region there is an intense activity of hydrocarbon extraction. Villahermosa has a density of 512 wells per 10 km^2 in the northwest of the area.

The climate is warm humid with abundant rains in summer, according to the Köppen classification, with average temperatures of 27.5 °C. Average annual rainfall of 1,992 mm [22].

On the other hand, the changes in land use became more notable at the same time as the discoveries of hydrocarbon deposits. In the period 2000–2008, the noteworthy loss of arboreal vegetation (1,624 ha) and wetlands (213 ha) began to be evident, while grassland (540 ha) and urban areas (1,334 ha) continued to increase. This trend of land-use change has been maintained (2008–2020), reaching 15,697 ha [23].

3 Data and Methods

3.1 Data

The SAR images used to implement the DInSAR technique in this work correspond to the Sentinel-1 satellite. These satellites operate in the *Interferometric Wide swath* (IW) imaging band mode and acquire data with a 250 km range at a spatial resolution of 5 × 20 m. IW captures three sub-swaths using the *Terrain Observation with Progressive Scans SAR* (TOPSAR) acquisition principle. IW products that are *Single Look Complex* (SLC) contain one image per sub-band and one for polarization channel, for a total of three images (single polarization) or six (dual polarization) in a single product [26]. Sentinel-1 images are available from its start of operation in 2014 (Sentinel-1A) until today.

Twenty-eight images from the Sentinel-1A satellite from 2014 to 2018 of the European Space Agency (obtained from https://search.asf.alaska.edu) were used.

The images were selected considering the following: 1) The perpendicular baseline between the image pair should be as small as possible, while smaller (closer to zero), the contribution of the topography component that is subtracted from the interferometric process is less. 2) The time interval between images, the shorter it is (less than 1,000 days), the less deco-relationship there will be for the scale of the movement that is to be measured [26, 27]. Using a DEM with good precision improves the quality of the phase by subtracting the topographic component. Sub-swath IW3 corresponding to Sentinel-1A descending orbit was processed.

Table 1 shows the image dates used for DInSAR processing. From these, 25 interferograms were formed.

3.2 Methods

The terrain's deformation was obtained with the implementation of a series of processes (see Fig. 2) that make up the DinSAR technique. Sentinel-1A images were processed with SNAP software (*Sentinel Application Platform*) to generate the interferograms. The interferograms were then unwrapped to obtain the interferometric phase with the SNAPHU algorithm (*Statistical-cost, Network-flow Algorithm for Phase Unwrapping*). Then, the terrain deformation rate was determined using SNAP software. For the cartographic output of the deformation, visualization, and interpretation, QGIS was used. Next, DInSAR processing will be described in more detail.

Image Co-registration. For interferometric processing, two or more images must be registered together. One image is selected as master and the others as slaves with dates after the first. The pixels in the slave images must be aligned with the master. This procedure ensures each pixel (of both images) belongs to the same location on the ground (in range and azimuth) [26].

Table 1. Sentinel-1A images used to form the interferometric pairs. Date: image acquisition date, T: images type (M: master, S: slave), B_L: perpendicular baseline, B_T: temporal baseline (frame: 99, path: 530, descending orbit).

Date	T	B_L	B_T	Date	T	B_L	B_T
2014-10-24	M			2017-04-11	S	29	192
2015-01-04	S	33	72	2017-05-05	M		
2015-05-04	S	11	192	2017-06-22	S	44	252
2015-06-21	S	−73	240	2017-10-08	S	18	360
2015-07-15	S	−159	264	2017-10-20	S	8	372
2015-08-08	S	−108	288	2017-11-01	S	30	384
2015-09-01	S	−112	312	2017-11-25	S	25	408
2015-10-19	S	−115	336	2017-12-07	S	−61	420
2016-10-13	M			2017-12-19	S	31	432
2016-11-30	S	44	48	2018-03-01	S	43	504
2016-12-24	S	16	72	2015-10-19	M		
2017-02-22	S	−15	132	2016-10-13	S	−5	361
2017-03-06	S	−98	144	2015-05-04	M		
2013-03-18	S	−35	156	2017-02-10	S	−33	648

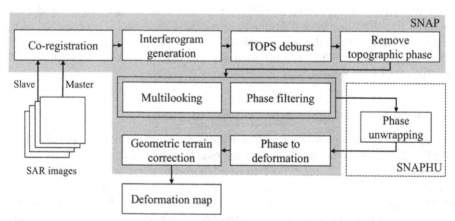

Fig. 2. Methodological scheme showing the procedures performed to implement the DInSAR technique and the software (SNAP, SNAPHU) used in each stage.

Interferogram Formation. The interferogram is formed by cross-multiplying the master image with the slave conjugate complex. The amplitudes of both images are multiplied while the phases are subtracted to form the interferogram [26]. Therefore, the interferogram is the phase variation between the two images and is related to the differences in object distances [19].

The integral DInSAR equation to calculate the interferometric phase, where M is the master image, and S is the slave image (1) [19]:

$$\Delta\varphi_{D\_Int} = \Delta\varphi_{Int} - \Delta\varphi_{Topo_{simu}}$$
$$= \Delta\varphi_{Displ} + \Delta\varphi_{Topo_{res}} + \Delta\varphi_{Atm_S} - \Delta\varphi_{Orb_S} - \Delta\varphi_{Orb_M} + \Delta\varphi_{Noise} + 2k\pi \tag{1}$$

Where:

$\Delta\varphi_{Int}$: Interferometric component.

$\Delta\varphi_{Topo_{simu}}$: Simulated topographic component, which implicitly contains a flat earth component.

$\Delta\varphi_{Topo_{res}}$: Component of the residual topographic error (RTE).

$\Delta\varphi_{Atm}$: Atmospheric phase component in the acquisition time of each image.

$\Delta\varphi_{Orb}$: Phase component due to orbital errors of each image.

$\Delta\varphi_{Noise}$: Phase noise.

$2k\pi$: Phase ambiguity (the result of the wrapped interferogram of $\Delta\varphi_{D\_Int}$).

The quality of the terrain deformation data obtained using the DInSAR technique depends on the quality of the differential interferometric phase [9].

The interferometric bands represent a 2π cycle of phase change. They appear on an interferogram as colored bands, where each represents a relative range difference of half the sensor wavelength. Relative ground motion can be calculated by counting the stripes and multiplying by half the wavelength [26].

The parameter called coherence ($0 <$ "coherence" < 1) is calculated to evaluate the interferometric phase. If the coherence is close to zero, it means that the scene is uncorrelated, and therefore the interferogram is noisy. Values close to 1 indicate high correlation, low noise on the interferogram, and a high-quality strain map [9]. Values less than 0.3 indicate that the phase estimates are too noisy to be used [27].

TOPS Deburst. Sentinel-1 images (due to the way they operate), present some bursts that cause noise and distortions to extract information. It is necessary to carry out this process TOPS deburst to eliminate such bursts [26].

Remove the Topographic Phase. The topographic phase's contribution is removed (Eq. 1) to disregard the components that do not contribute to the phase to obtain terrain deformation. For this, a well-known DEM is used to simulate the reference DEM based interferogram, in this case, the DEM SRTM1 (*Shuttle Radar Topography Mission*) [26, 27].

Multilooking. It is done to decrease the noise of the interferogram. It consists of obtaining the average of the pixels in each direction (several looks) in the interferograms. Interferograms of approximately 14 m^2 were obtained [9, 28].

Phase Filtering. Subsequently, the Goldstein filter was performed, a pre-processing technique that reduces noise from the interferometric phase, facilitating its development in terms of precision [29]. By completing this filtering, the interferometric strips are accentuated and become sharper.

Phase unwrapping. In the interferogram, the interferometric phase is ambiguous and is only known within 2π. The phase must first be unwrapped to separate the interferometric phase from the topographic height [26].

Starting from the phase and amplitude information (see Fig. 3), the phase unwrapping is performed using the SNAPHU algorithm. SNAPHU is a statistical cost network flow algorithm for phase development developed at Stanford University [30] as a complement to the SNAP software developed by ESA and freely available. The focus of radar interferometry in this step is to work with the two-dimensional relative phase signal, the modulus 2π of the absolute phase signal (unknown). In this sense, the biggest drawback is the wrapped phase given in an interval of $(-\pi, \pi)$ and, on the other hand, the phase unwrapping, being more complex due to its non-linearity and non-singularity [31].

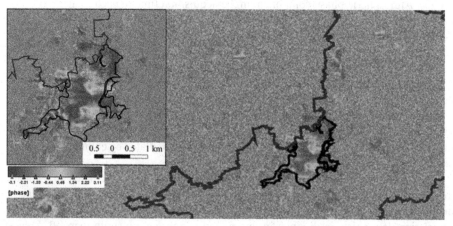

Fig. 3. Filtered interferogram. Sub-swath IW3 corresponding to the pair of images on 2014-10-13 and 2015-01-04. The polygon in brown shows the limits of Municipality Centro and the black one, the Villahermosa city boundary. (Color figure online)

Phase to deformation conversion. In this step, the unwrapped interferometric phase is converted to heights. The phase of several discrete heights is calculated and compared to the actual phase of the interferogram to determine the height. An external DEM is used as a reference (SRTM 1 Arc-Second) [29–31].

Geometric correction of the terrain. Geometric correction or geocoding converts a slope range image or terrain range geometry to a map coordinate system. Besides, the use of a DEM is required to correct the mentioned distortions [31].

Land deformation map. As the last step, the terrain deformation map is obtained in cm/year, and this is taken to the Geographic Information System for better visualization and interpretation of this [9, 26, 28, 30].

4 Results and Discussion

Six of the 25 interferograms formed (see Fig. 4) and their respective coherence maps obtained from 2014 to 2018 (see Fig. 5) are represented. The thresholds obtained in the coherence maps were very similar, ranging from 0.01 to 0.992, with an approximate mean of 0.25 to 3.

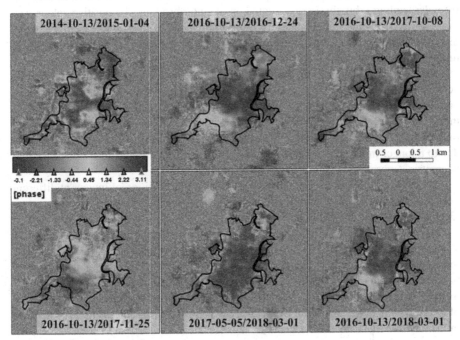

Fig. 4. Flattened interferograms of the city of Villahermosa that contain information on topography and terrain deformation for the period 2014-10-13 to 2018-03-01.

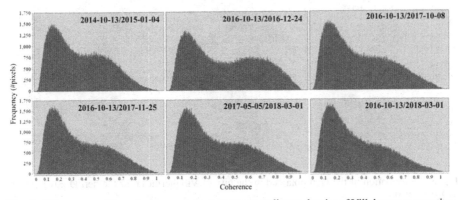

Fig. 5. Histograms of the coherence parameter corresponding to the city of Villahermosa covering the period 2014-10-13 to 2018-03-01.

Acceptable results were obtained from the 25 processed interferograms in the image pairs shown in Fig. 4. The contribution of those, as mentioned earlier, temporal and atmospheric distortions, were detected in the interferograms. In an interferogram, the deformation pattern is shown with a color cycle. Each stripe represents a change in the distance from the satellite to the ground, which is equal to half the radar wavelength. When the number of stripes visible on the interferogram is multiplied by half the wavelength, a relative displacement of the points can be estimated. Since the images used are from descending orbit, this is represented on the interferograms by positive values (see Fig. 4). Negative values in the interferograms correspond to sinks, while positive values represent the uprisings [32]. Interference stripes with the same color within the cycle represent the same relative deformation.

The average coherence of the interferometric phase for processed images was between 0.3 and 0.40 (see Fig. 5). The highest coherence values belong to interferograms of 2016-10-13 to 2016-12-24 and 2016-10-13 to 2018-03-01 with 0.40 and 0.35 thresholds, respectively. Thresholds values greater than 0.3, indicate areas with similar reflection characteristics. On the other hand, the areas with values less than 0.3 may be due to a longer time interval between the two image acquisitions, the temporal, spatial geometric decorrelation between the two SAR images [14].

Despite the temporal decorrelations caused by the acquisition of images at different year seasons and with a temporality of 648 days, the deformation results were consistent (3 to 15 cm/year from 2014-10-13 to 2018-03-01).

From 2014-10-13 to 2015-01-04, the city of Villahermosa had a sinking rate of 4 cm/year. From 2016-10-13 to 2018-03-01, the subsidence rate was 15 cm/year. The lowest subsidence values corresponded to the interferograms with a smaller temporal baseline. The areas affected by the sinking phenomenon increased from 327 ha from 2014 to 2015, to 6,232 ha from 2014 to 2018. Urban expansion and the continued exploitation of hydrocarbon wells contribute to this increase in the sinking rate from 2014 to 2018 in the city of Villahermosa (see Fig. 6).

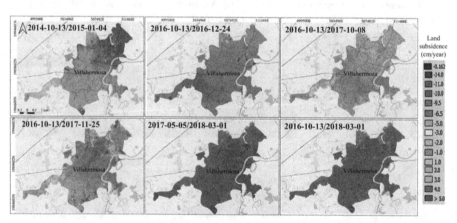

Fig. 6. Deformation of the land obtained in the city of Villahermosa for the period 2014-10-13 to 2018-03-01.

5 Conclusions and Future Work

The traditional DInSAR technique that obtains the deformation of the terrain from pairs of SAR images is viable for measuring and quantifying the evolution of the subsidence in urban areas at different periods. From 2014-10-13 to 2015-01-04, subsidence in the city of Villahermosa had a sinking rate of 4 cm/year. For the period from 2016-10-13 to 2018-03-01, the subsidence rate increased to 15 cm/year. The lowest subsidence values corresponded to the interferograms with the smallest time scale. Atmospheric and temporal distortions contributed to the erroneous development of interferograms. These led to incoherent interferometric phases to obtain the terrain deformation. The areas affected by the subsidence phenomenon increased from 327 ha (2014-2015) to 6,232 ha (2016-2018).

This work is part of an ongoing investigation on subsidence in the Tabasco and Campeche coastal plain. As future work, control points will be obtained in the field, as well as from the INEGI geodetic network, to validate the obtained results. Since there have been no previous studies to monitor subsidence in this region, it is necessary to quantify it to prevent and reduce the region's vulnerability to this phenomenon and other associated ones, such as floods and coastal erosion.

Acknowledgments. The authors would like to thank the Interdisciplinary Center of Marine Sciences of the National Polytechnic Institute (CICIMAR-IPN) for the support to carry out this work (through the project SIP-20195187 *Coastal subsidence assessment in the Mexican states of Tabasco and Campeche using DInSAR*). Thanks also to the three anonymous reviewers for their valuable comments, and to Alaska Satellite Facility Distributed Active Archive Center (ASF DAAC) for providing access to Sentinel-1A imagery.

References

1. Keller, E.A., Blodget, R.H.: Riesgos Naturales. Procesos de la Tierra como riesgos, desastres y catástrofes. 1st edn. Pearson Prentice Hall, Madrid (2004)
2. Tomás, R., Herrera, G., Delgado, J., Peña, F.: Subsidencia del terreno. Enseñanza de la Ciencia de la Tierra **17**(3), 295–302 (2009)
3. Vázquez, N.J., de Justo J.L.: La subsidencia en Murcia. Implicaciones y consecuencias en la edificación. In: COPOT, pp. 1–260, Murcia, España (2002)
4. Dávila-Hernández, N.A., Madrigal-Uribe, D.: Aplicación de interferometría radar en el estudio de subsidencia en el Valle de Toluca, México. Rev. Cien. Espaciales **8**(1), 294–309 (2015)
5. Riel, B., Simons, M., Pontl, D., Agram, P., Jolivet, R.: Quantifying ground deformation in the los angeles and santa ana coastal basins due to groundwater withdrawal. Water Resour. Res. **54**, 3557–3582 (2018)
6. Hay-Man, A., Ge, L., Du, Z., Wang, S., Ma, Ch.: Satellite radar interferometric for monitoring subsidence induced by longwall mining activity using Radarsat-2, Sentinel-1 and ALOS-2 data. Appl. Earth Obs. Geoinform. **61**, 92–103 (2017)
7. Temporim, F.A., Gama, F.F., Mura, J.C., Paradella, W.R., Silva, G.G.: Application of persistent scatterers interferometry for surface displacements monitoring in N5E open pit iron mine using TerraSAR-X data, in Carajás Province, Amazon region. Braz. J. Geol. **47**(2), 225–235 (2017)

8. Liu, F., et al.: Inferring geothermal reservoir processes at the Raft River geothermal field, Idaho, USA, through modeling InSAR-measured surface deformation. J. Geophys. Res. Solid Earth **123**, 3645–3666 (2018)
9. Sarychikhina, O., Glowacha, E., Suárez, F., Mellors, R., Hernández, R.: Aplicación de DInSAR a los estudios de subsidencia en el Valle de Mexicali. Boletín de la Sociedad Geológica Mexicana **63**(1), 1–13 (2011)
10. Higgins, S.A., Overeem, I., Steckler, M.S., Syvitski, J.P.M., Seeber, L., Akhter, S.H.: InSAR measurements of compaction and subsidence in the Ganges-Brahmaputra Delta, Bangladesh. J. Geophys. Res. Earth Surf. **119**, 1768–1781 (2014)
11. Saleh, M., Becker, M.: New estimation of Nile Delta subsidence rates from InSAR and GPS analysis. Environ. Earth Sci. **78**(6), 1–12 (2019)
12. Jones, A.E., An, K., Blom, R.G., Kent, J.D., Ivins, E.R., Bekaert, D.: Anthropogenic and geologic influences on subsidence in the vicinity of New Orleans, Lousiana. J. Geophys. Res. Soild Earth **121**, 3867–3887 (2016)
13. Cianflone, G., Tolomei, C., Brunori, C.A., Dominici, R.: InSAR time series analysis of natural and anthropogenic coastal plain subsidence (Southern Italy). Remote Sens. **7**, 16004–160023 (2015)
14. Arenas, I., Hernández, B., Royero, G., Cioce, V., Wildermann, E.: Detección de subsidencia por efecto de extracción petrolera aplicando la técnica DInSAR en Venezuela. Rev. Mapp. **28**(195), 8–26 (2019)
15. Ketelaar, G., et al.: Integrated monitoring of subsidence due to hydrocarbon production: consolidating the foundation. Int. Assoc. Hydrol. Sci. **382**, 117–123 (2020)
16. Herrera, G., et al.: Advanced DInSAR analysis on mining areas: La Union case study (Murcia, SE Spain). Eng. Geol. **90**, 148–159 (2007)
17. Sillerico, E., Marchamalo, M., Rejas, J.G., Martínez, R.: La técnica DInSAR: bases y aplicación a la medición de subsidencias del terreno en la construcción. Informes de la Construcción **62**(519), 47–53 (2010)
18. Bürgmann, R., Rosen, P.A., Fielding, E.: Synthetic aperture radar interferometric to measure earth surface and its deformation. Earth Planet Sci. Lett. **28**, 169–209 (2000)
19. Crosetto, M., Monserrat, O., Cuevas-González, M., Devanthéry, N., Crippa, B.: Persistent scatterer interferometry: a review. ISPRS J. Photogram. Remote Sens. **115**, 78–89 (2016)
20. Li, Z., Zou, W., Ding, X., Chen, Y., Liu, G.: A quantitative measure for the quality of INSAR interferograms based on phase differences. Photogram. Eng. Remote Sens. **70**(10), 1131–1137 (2004)
21. Constantini, F., Ruescas, A.B.: Estimación de la subsidencia en el área de Ostrava (República Checa) utilizando datos ERS SAR con técnicas de Interferometría Diferencial. Teledetección: Agua y desarrollo sostenible. In: XIII Congreso de la Asociación Española de Teledetección, pp. 545–548, Teledetección: Agua y desarrollo sostenible, España (2009)
22. Galindo, A.A., Ruiz A.S., Morales, H.A., Sánchez, L., Carrizales, E., Villegas P.C.: Atlas de Riesgos del Municipio de Centro. H. Ayuntamiento Constitucional de Centro, Tabasco. In: Servicios Integrales de Ingeniería y Calidad SA de CV, pp. 43–67, México (2015)
23. Palomeque, M.A., Galindo, A., Sánchez, A.L., Escalona, M.J.: Pérdida de humedales y vegetación por urbanización en la cuenca del río Grijalva, México. Investigaciones Geográficas **68**, 151–172 (2017)
24. Capdepont-Ballina, J.L., Marín-Olán, P.: La economía de Tabasco y su impacto en el crecimiento urbano de la ciudad de Villahermosa (1960-2010). Revista LiminaR Estudios Sociales y Humanísticos **12**(1), 144–160 (2014)
25. INEGI: Síntesis de Información Geográfica del Estado de Tabasco, (Digital). Aguascalientes, México, pp. 25–32 (2001)
26. Meyer, F.: Sentinel-1 InSAR processing using the Sentinel-1 toolbox. In: Adapted from Coursework Developed in Alaska Satellite Facility, pp. 1–21 (2019)

27. Ferretti, A., Monti-Guarnieri, A., Prati, C., Rocca, F.: InSAR Principles: Guidelines for SAR Interferometry Processing and Interpretation TM-19, pp. 1–63. ESA, France (2007)

28. Seppi, S.: Uso de Interferometría Diferencial para monitorear deformaciones del terreno en la comuna de Córdova, provincia de Bolzano, Italia. Grado de Máser en aplicaciones espaciales de alerta y respuesta temprana a emergencias. Universidad Nacional de Córdova, p. 32 (2016)

29. Golstein, R.M., Warner, C.L.: Radar interferogram filtering for geophysical applications. Geophys. Res. Lett. **25**(21), 4035–4038 (1998)

30. Chen, C.W., Zebker, H.A.: Phase unwrapping for large SAR interferograms: statistical segmentation and generalized network models. IEEE Trans. Geosci. Remote Sens. **18**(40), 338–351 (2002)

31. Guerrero, C.A., Hernández, P.A.: Determinación de un modelo digital de elevación a partir de imágenes de radar Sentinel-1usando interferometría SAR. In: Proyecto curricular de Ingeniería Catastral y Geodesia, pp. 45–110, Bogotá, Colombia (2017)

32. Hanssen, R.F.: Radar Interferometry. Data Interpretation and Error Analysis. Remote sensing and Digital Image Processing. 2nd edn. Kluwer Academic Publishers, The Netherlands (2002)

A Proposal for Semantic Integration of Crime Data in Mexico City

Francisco Carrillo-Brenes[1]([⊠]), Luis M. Vilches-Blázquez[2], and Félix Mata[1]

[1] Instituto Politécnico Nacional, Unidad Profesional Interdisciplinaria en Ingeniería y
Tecnologías Avanzadas, Mexico City, Mexico
f.carrillo.brenes@gmail.com, mmatar@ipn.mx
[2] Instituto Politécnico Nacional, Centro de Investigación en Computación, Mexico City, Mexico
lmvilches@cic.ipn.mx

Abstract. Crime is a common problem in big cities where the authorities regularly update data crime reports. In Mexico City, the crime reports are available as open data. However, other relevant data are not connected to them (e.g., socioeconomic data). Therefore, the socioeconomic and geographic data can help understand how the crime is characterized and what social indicators are related to it. In this research, we explore how data crime reports are described and how they can be associated in an Ontology with other data, such as socioeconomic and geographic data. The goal is to discover the social indicators related to a particular crime in a specific area by using SPARQL queries from a knowledge representation. Then, data sets from crime reports, socioeconomic and geographic data from 2016 were integrated to explore crime behavior in Mexico City. The work uses a NeOn methodology in which resources from existing ontologies or non-ontological resources can be mixed. Next, a set of SPARQL queries is defined to extract the knowledge from ontology and discover the associations between crime in geographic and socioeconomic domains. The results showed a set of queries where it is possible to know where a crime occurred and what other factors are associated with the crime and help to identify possible patterns among them.

Keywords: Crime data · Mixed data · Behavior crime data · Ontology

1 Introduction

Crime occurrence is a phenomenon that affects the geographic area and its inhabitants. Impacting the status of the area, the living of the inhabitants, and how they make decisions. Today, data crime incidence is generated and published as open data in Mexico City. Institutions and organizations use this information to treat and understand the phenomena from different perspectives.

The traditional approach to generating and storing the crime reports consists of schemas of data (files and databases), limiting the capability to retrieve the relevant information, identifying associations, or combining the information with other data sources to reveal trends and patterns. Thus, a knowledge representation model (ontology) can

© Springer Nature Switzerland AG 2020
M. F. Mata-Rivera et al. (Eds.): GIS LATAM 2020, CCIS 1276, pp. 30–48, 2020.
https://doi.org/10.1007/978-3-030-59872-3_3

be built to represent the crime reports; it could improve the access and retrieve the relevant data to identify the associations and patterns. It generates that the original dataset's interoperability is increased.

In this work, data from three domains are integrated socioeconomic, geographic, and crime to reveal associations. Crime reports and socioeconomic data can be transformed into knowledge, represented using the knowledge representation model [1]. The ontology is the model used in this work, which is defined as a formal, explicit specification of a shared conceptualization' [2]. It represents formal knowledge as a set of concepts of a domain using a vocabulary. This vocabulary is used to declare the types, properties, and relations between the concepts.

The dataset of crime reports from Mexico City is described as an ontology; it was developed based on scenario-based methodology. These scenarios emphasize the join, re-engineering, and reuse of ontological and non-ontological resources. Ontology is built using Protégé [available at https://protege.stanford.edu/], using the resources to define the concepts of the dataset, the properties, and relations.

The ontology can be used to develop an RDF file, where the dataset is described as semantic triples which is represented in the form subject-predicate-object expressions. Also, this RDF was published in a server, in order to make queries and retrieve data from the file. These queries were made using a particular language, which is SPARQL. This language is used to retrieve and also RDF management, like data creation, modification, and erase.

The rest of the paper is organized as follows: related work is presented in Sect. 2, while in Sect. 3, the datasets used are described. Section 4 the development methodology used in this work, and Sect. 5 shows the conclusions and future work.

2   Related Work

This section presents some works related to using an ontology to describe crime data and its analysis.

In [3], Jalil et al. used violent crimes as crime variables. The software TopBraid Composer was used to develop the ontology, defining relations and attributes. The ontology was used to implement a prototype named CrimeAnalysis, in which data about a new case is introduced and matches the preexisting data in the model. In the current work for the ontology development was used Protégé and for the RDF was used Python. When a query is made in this research, socioeconomic data related to an area where a crime occurred, is retrieved.

In [4], the data source were newspaper articles. The author obtained entities from the articles using natural language processing techniques. The ontology was developed using the entities extracted, and they added other existing ontologies. In the current work, the data source is obtained from an open data repository.

While in [5], a new ontology was developed named SMONT. Its primary purpose was to solve crimes. Its data source were complaints found in social networks, and these were extracted with natural language processing. Besides, the authors used open data repositories as a data source. The ontology was developed with the NeOn methodology, and the software used is Protégé. They used the ontology as a search tool for a kind of crime with SPARQL queries. The current work is similar, both use crime reports as a data source, but in the current work, socioeconomic data was added as an additional data source. The ontology development was made following the NeOn methodology and with Protégé software, and with the queries is possible to retrieve spatial-temporal characteristics and the socioeconomic characteristics.

In [6], the authors used the crime reports from social media and news. From there, they extracted entities using NLP techniques. With entities extracted and defined, the possible relations between them were recognized and declared in the ontology development. They developed the ontology using TopBraid. The current work uses official crime reports. The recognition of entities is made in the official data.

In [7], an existing ontology was adapted to the crime domain. The entities added to this ontology about crime were extracted from documents using natural language processing, specifically with an algorithm named SVO (Subject, Verb, Object) to analyze sentences to construct triples. In the current work, the ontology is made from scratch, reusing some concepts from other ontologies, and the entities are defined from the dataset.

While in [8], the authors made an extension to [5]. They used official crime reports and extractions from social networks. Subsequently, they extended the ontology SMONT with new classes extracted from the database compressing the crime reports from police and social networks. They built a knowledge base and applied machine learning to identify patterns according to a crime classification. In the current work, there will also be a union of the crime reports and the extraction from social networks, but in the part of classification and pattern detection, deep learning will be used.

In [9], the authors developed an ontological knowledge base reusing an event ontology for criminal events and causes. The events were extracted from news headlines using NLP techniques. Criminal events are extracted from the official crime reports from the city, and the ontology development reuses some existing ontologies in the current research.

Another ontology to describe criminal events was developed in [10]. The authors extracted news related to criminal events from several web pages and with NLP techniques extracted the entities and separated the entities per crime. With these entities, they developed the ontology to describe the selected crimes. In contrast, the current work used official crime reports from an open data repository, and the entities were extracted from there, besides the use of socioeconomic data to relate the crime reports with the social indicators.

In Korea, Gun-woo et al. [11] developed an ontology, based on information extracted from official reports and unstructured data regarding intrusion theft, and they implemented an ontology-based search service. In the current work, the ontology was developed from the official reports, and it was added socioeconomic indicators to find a relation between them. The publication in Virtuoso allows performing queries of a specific crime and retrieve indicators related.

3 Data Sources and Wrangling

Data used in this research consist of two datasets:

1. The first dataset is the investigation folders of the attorney general's office of the city of Mexico (available at http://datos.cdmx.gob.mx/explore/dataset/carpetas-de-investigacion-pgj-de-la-ciudad-de-mexico/). Its license is CC BY, which allows the user to share and adapt the dataset. It contains reports made by crime victims in many dependencies in Mexico City. In the crimes reported, 292 different crimes occurred in the 16 mayoralties in the city and some municipalities of Mexico's state.
2. The second dataset is the social backwardness index, which is issued by, institute for measuring the social development in Mexico (CONEVAL by acronym in spanish) available at https://www.coneval.org.mx/Medicion/IRS/Paginas/Indice_Rezago_Social_2015.aspx). The license of the dataset is CC BY. It contains indicators as total population, illiteracy rate, percentage of people not attending the school, and percentage of people with primary education incomplete, among others.

The data wrangling process [12] was performed into both datasets. It consists of extracting, cleaning, and integrating with other datasets. Moreover, the identification and datatypes of each useful variable are achieved.

The crime dataset contains 292 crimes, some crimes with a low number of reports. Then, we selected the crimes with more than 2000 reports, obtaining only 27 crimes as follows: confidence abuse, sexual abuse, threats, third party property damage to an automobile, intentional property damage, facts complain, dispossession, documents forgery, fraud, injuries in a collision, intentional injuries, drug dealing, home theft without violence, violent business theft, nonviolent business theft, vehicle driver theft, subway passenger nonviolent theft, cellphone violent theft, cellphone nonviolent theft, violent theft on a public road, vehicle accessories theft, object theft, theft of objects from inside a vehicle, violent vehicle theft, vehicle nonviolent theft, identity usurpation, and family violence.

In addition, were maintained only the reports concerning Mexico City, i.e., the 16 mayoralties of Mexico City. The dataset resulting had 144082 tuples for the year 2016. It has 15 variables, including the datatype containing the coordinates where crime reported occurred. Eleven variables are text type. These variables include occurrence month, crime reported, crime type, prosecution, agency, research unity, mayoralty where the crime occurred, suburb, streets, and a Geopoint, which is the union of the coordinates. There is a variable with date datatype, which is when the crime occurred, and the last variable refers to the year.

The second dataset picked, the social backwardness index includes data about people. This dataset has values for five different years, 2000, 2005, 2010, 2015, and 2020. In this work, the data of 2015 was maintained, and the other removed because the crime data is of 2016. There are five variables in the dataset; all of them have a numeric datatype, specifically, float datatype. The variables are the number of people living in an area, the illiteracy rate, the percentage of people between 6 and 14 years old not attending the school, and the percentage of people without access to health services, and the percentage of people 15 years older with primary education incomplete.

Both datasets, the crime reports, were integrated into one dataset using Python and Pandas library. The social data was added in new columns per each mayoralty found in the crime dataset, resulting in a dataset with 20 variables and the 144082 tuples.

4 Methodology

The methodology consists of three phases: 1) building an ontology to describe crime and socioeconomic data following the NeOn [13] methodology. 2) RDF publication and queries construction to knowledge extraction of ontology 3) Identifying patterns from the results obtained by queries. It is represented in Fig. 1.

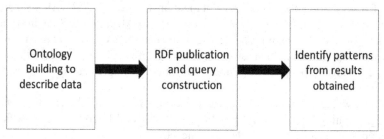

Fig. 1. Methodology

4.1 NeOn Methodology

NeOn methodology is used to build the ontology. It considers the existence of ontologies related, the collaborative development of ontologies, the dynamic dimension, the reuse, and the re-engineering of the knowledge resources. Nine scenarios compose it, which a brief description of each one is the following:

Scenario one: "from specification to implementation," refers to ontology development from scratch, where the ontology requirements are specified: scope, the possible end-users, the dataset specifications, and competency questions. Besides, possible ontologies to reuse must be identified according to the datasets and the design of the URI-base, which is the identifier for the entire ontology.

Scenario 2, named reusing and re-engineering non-ontological resources, refers to deciding which resources can be reused in the ontology building and transforming those resources into ontologies. Scenario 3: Reusing ontological resources, refers to the use of existing ontologies, as a whole, as a module or as a statement.

In scenario 4, reusing and re-engineering ontological resources, existing ontologies can be reused and re-engineered before their integration in the new ontology. While in scenario 5 and 6 are similar called: reusing and merging ontological resources, the ontology developers reuse and merge existing ontologies to create a new ontology. In scenario 7: reusing ontology design patterns, it is designed patterns repositories to reduce modeling decisions. Scenario 8 "ontological resources" consists of restructuring existing ontologies and integrating them into the new ontology.

The scenario 9: localizing ontological resources, refers to translating the ontology developed in other languages to obtain a multilingual ontology.

These scenarios described can be combined in different ways.

4.2 Ontology Modeling

In this research, from NeOn [13] scenarios described in Subsect. 4.1, scenarios 1, 2, 3, 6, and 8 were used.

In scenario 1, the competency questions were defined. These questions are the ones that the ontology will answer; the questions must be according to the domain to describe. In our research, the domain is criminal incidence and socioeconomic data. Some of these questions are the following:

- How many crimes are registered?
- Where occurred a crime?
- When occurred a crime?
- Is there a socioeconomic indicator in a region?
- How many people live in a region?
- How many different crimes are there?
- What is the social indicator relating to a crime?
- What are the coordinates of a crime reported?
- Where there are more crimes reported?

The next step is to recognize the possible ontological and non-ontological resources used in ontology development. The ontological resources refer to ontologies already developed or some statements from ontologies regarding the development domain, which can describe the data and help answer the competency questions. Secondly, non-ontological resources refer to a knowledge resource that is not included or formalized in an ontology. In our work, it includes definitions of different crimes in crime reports dataset and definitions of some variables in the socioeconomic data and information of the region where the crimes occurred. The ontologies selected are shown in Table 1.

Table 1. Existing ontologies used.

Prefix	Meaning
QB	Vocabulary for data cube representation
QB4ST	Vocabulary for data cube representation with spatial temporal attributes
GEO	Geographic ontology
DBO	Dbpedia ontology

The explanation of each one element in Table 1 is the following:

- QB (available at https://www.w3.org/TR/vocab-data-cube/). Since the dataset is a relational database, this can be presented or modeled as an OLAP, and this ontology allows it to represent information from a table using the W3C RDF standard. It is focused purely on the publication of multi-dimensional data on the web.
- QB4ST (available at https://www.w3.org/TR/qb4st/). Is the ontology used to describe a data cube with attributes spatial-temporal. This ontology is an extension to QB ontology. It is used to define spatial-temporal attributes and measures.

- Geo (available at https://www.w3.org/2003/01/geo/). Since the data has longitude and latitude variables, the ontology used to represent coordinates was the geo vocabulary from W3C. This ontology is a *basic* RDF vocabulary that provides the Semantic Web community with a namespace for representing latitude, longitude, and other information about spatially-located things.
- DBO (available at http://dbpedia.org/). DBpedia resources were used to define some values of the socioeconomic data in the ontology. DBpedia is a project to export resources from Wikimedia to the semantic web, and it contains ontological resources.

The non-ontological resources were definitions of crimes, location information, and definitions regarding socioeconomic variables found in the social backwardness dataset. Moreover, the datasets used had metadata, which defines the names used in the datasets. Metadata was used to declare concepts in the ontology and establish relations between those concepts.

There are not ontologies to describe the crime in repositories. Thus, the classes and subclasses used to describe crime reports were defined using metadata. These classes include crime, crime category, prosecution, year, month, date, agency, location, population, and health services. The classes defined using metadata are shown in Table 2.

Table 2. Classes defined

Classes	Subclasses
Crime	
Category	
Prosecution	
Year	
Month	
Date	
Location	Mayoralty Suburb Street
Population	
Health services	
Agency	
Research unity	

Also, relations were defined using the dataset's metadata. The object properties defined with metadata and the data properties defined using the dataset include "hasIncompleteEducation" or "attendsSchool" are shown in Table 3.

For each property, a domain and a range had to be defined. Domain refers to the resource that has the property, and the range is the literal or resource that is affected by

Table 3. Object and data properties defined in the ontology

Object properties	Data properties
hasAgency	withoutHealth
hasCategory	attendsSchool
hasProsecution	incompleteEducation
hasDate	
hasLocation	
hasGeopoint	
hasResearchUnit	

the first resource. Most of the object properties defined have crime class as the domain and range different resources, while data properties defined has location as the domain.

Applying scenario 2, the non-ontological resources were picked, like crime definitions or places information, are integrated into the ontology or the dataset. Also, information about social indicators used was added and integrated to the original dataset.

In scenario 3, the ontological resources were picked. The existing ontologies added are shown in Table 1. These ontologies fit in the development, but not entirely. Besides, scenario six is also used, which refers, as mentioned, to reuse, re-engineering, and merge the ontological resources.

Now, applying scenario 6, the ontologies selected in scenario three (shown in Table 1) are modified to fit the new ontology and, subsequently, merge them with the new. The modifications were made in the conceptualization level. QB ontology was imported in this development entirely. As mentioned, a relational database can be described as an OLAP in the ontology. Thus, the entire classes and properties are imported into the new ontology.

In this, QB4ST is added too, also entirely, because the dataset used has attributes and measures spatial-temporal. In comparison, GEO ontology is imported entirely because this ontology has only classes to describe the coordinates.

The DBpedia ontology was imported, but this one has many resources and properties to use in an ontology. From this ontology, only one class was imported, which is "PopulatedPlace." This class was used to define the location class defined previously. Also, from this ontology, two data properties were used: population total, which describes the number of people living in a place, and this data property is used to relate location and populated place classes. Moreover, the other data property used was illiteracy rate, which refers to the percentage of people in a place with illiteracy; this property relates the location with a percentage value.

The last scenario picked, which is scenario 8 consists of three activities, modularization, pruning, and enrichment. In this ontology to describe the crime and social data, the prune was used to remove relations and attributes of the imported ontologies, especially from DBpedia ontology. Besides, two activities presented in the enrichment were made, the extension and specialization. In the first one, the ontology is extended with new concepts from the ontologies imported. In the second activity, the ontology is refined and specializes in specific concepts and relations.

All the classes defined with the ontologies imported are shown in Fig. 2.

Fig. 2. Defined classes

While in Fig. 3 the entire object properties are shown.

The data properties defined to describe the dataset are shown in Fig. 4.

The crime class was defined with a set of axioms like something that always has a category, always has a date, always has a mayoralty location, on occasions has coordinates, on occasions has a second street.

In contrast, Location is always a populated place, a mayoralty, is divided into suburbs and streets. Besides, a location is always a populated place, has a population, has an illiteracy rate. The total axioms of the ontology, between the declared and the already declared in the ontologies imported, are 476 axioms.

Fig. 3. Defined object properties

Fig. 4. Defined data properties

4.3 RDF Generation

Subsequently, an RDF file was developed, importing the ontology developed and the complete dataset containing the crime reports and the socioeconomic data. file. Using Python and the RDFlib library, an empty graph was defined, in which the triplets defining the data are added one by one.

The dataset was described as a data cube in the ontology developed. First, the definition as a datacube is added on the graph. At first, URI identifiers for each cube component were defined for the cube, dataset, cube properties, and components specifications. Next, the cube's measures and dimensions were defined. Definitions were made with classes in data cube ontology and with data cube for Spatio-temporal ontology.

Data related to the crime were defined as dimensions, the crime itself, prosecution, category, agency, and research unit. Also, location with its subclasses, i.e., the mayoralties, suburbs, and streets were defined as dimensions in the cube. The month of the report and the date of each report in the dataset were defined as temporal dimensions Using a data cube with Spatio-temporal data.

While the values about the socioeconomic like population, illiteracy, were defined as measures; the latitude and longitude coordinates were defined as spatial measures. In parallel, while the cube properties are being defined, the dataset is defined with the ontology developed, specifically with the classes and properties defined for crime reports.

Then, as the location of a crime is defined as a dimension property with the data cube part, it is also defined as a populated place, and his populations are described according to the data properties declared before. Crime is declared as a dimension property and also is declared as an instance of Crime class and the relations with the prosecution, the agency, the location, and its definition using isDefinedBy from RDF-schema.

With the declaration of each dimension, the next step was to define the data cube structure. Subsequently, the observations were defined, which is considered in the data cube ontology as the actual data, i.e., the observations are the tuples of the dataset. Each tuple is added in the graph, defining the number of the observation and appending all the data to its corresponding class of the ontology.

4.4 SPARQL Queries

The last part of this RDF development is the publication of the knowledge base, to make queries over the data in a semantic way with SPARQL language [14] using Virtuoso software [available at http://vos.openlinksw.com/owiki/wiki/VOS]. In this software, the RDF is uploaded, and with SPARQL, specific data in the RDF can be retrieved.

One query written in SPARQL language is shown below, in this, it was retrieved the mayoralty, the suburb and the population of each mayoralty.

Prefix nsl: <http://localhost:8890/cubos/carpetas/prop>
Prefix owl: <http://www.w3.org/2002/07/owl#>
Prefix qb: <http://purl.org/linked-data(cube#>
Prefix rdf: <http://www.w3.org/1999/02/22-rdf-syntax-ns#>
Select ?Mayoralty ?Suburb ?Population
Where

```
{
?obs rdf:type qb:Observation;
ns1:alcaldia ?Mayoralty;
ns1:colonia ?Suburb;
ns1:población ?Population.
}
Group by ?Mayoralty
```

The result of the query is a table showing the number of inhabitants per mayoralty and the suburbs per mayoralty. A fragment of the table obtained in the query is shown in Table 4.

Table 4. Population per mayoralty

Mayoralty	Suburb	Population
Benito Juárez	San José Insurgentes	391939
Álvaro Obregón	Tetelpan	746887
Azcapotzalco	Aldana	400708
Benito Juárez	Del Carmen	391939
Coyoacán	Barrio San Lucas	609627
Coyoacán	Prado Churubusco	609627
Coyoacán	Paseos de Taxqueña	609627
Álvaro Obregón	Central Camionera poniente	746887

In addition, other **Queries made in the RDF** are: Q1 = {Crime counting per mayoralty}, Q2 = {Crime counting per suburb}, Q3 = {Crime counting per crime}, Q4 = {Illiteracy rate}, Q5 = {Percentage of people with incomplete education}, Q6 = {Crime more reported in mayoralties and illiteracy rate}, Q7 = {Highest Illiteracy rate and the crime more reported} and Q8 = {Lowest illiteracy rate and crime with more reports}

Query Q1, allows to know the crimes per mayoralty in Mexico City, where Cuauhtemoc mayoralty had the highest numbers of reports with 23027 crimes reported in 2016. The next mayoralty is Iztapalapa with 21129 reports, followed by Gustavo A. Madero with 13359 and Benito Juaréz, where 13333 crimes were reported. In contrast, the mayoralty with the lowest number of crimes reported is Milpa Alta, which has 783 reports, preceded by La Magdalena Contreras with 2350 reports and Tlahuac with 3007 crimes reported. It is shown in the map of Fig. 5.

The zones with more crimes reported in Mexico city are colored in yellow and white, the crimes reported in other zones are colored in red, while the fewer crimes reported are colored in blue. As can be seen, all the mayoralties have suffered a crime.

In Q2, the crime reports per suburb distribution was retrieved. In the results, the suburbs with the highest number of reports were recognized. Some of them are in mayoralties

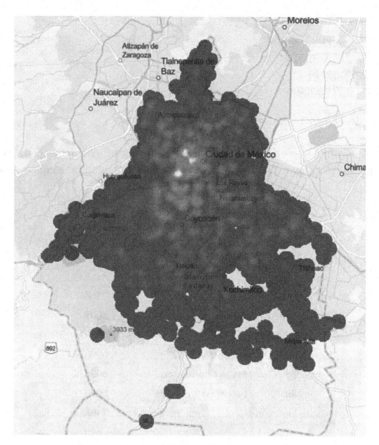

Fig. 5. Crime distribution (Color figure online)

with more crimes reported like Centro suburb, which had 4426 reports, or Doctores suburb with 2653 reports. Both located in Cuauhtémoc Mayoralty, which, as mentioned, is the mayoralty with the highest number of reports

The number of reports per crime was retrieved in query Q3, and the resulting table is shown in Table 5.

The crime with the highest reports in the data is domestic violence. At the same time, the crime with the lowest number of reports is subway passenger nonviolent theft with 620 reports.

Q4 was performed to retrieve the illiteracy rate of each mayoralty. The results show that Milpa Alta mayoralty is the one with the highest value, which is 3.31%, the second mayoralty is Iztapalapa with 2.37%. In contrast, the mayoralty with the lowest illiteracy rate is Benito Juárez, which value is 0.29, preceded by Miguel Hidalgo and Cuauhtémoc with 0.86 and 1.09, respectively. The results obtained were transformed into a map layer, shown in Fig. 6.

In which, each mayoralty is colored in a scale to indicate the region's illiteracy rate. The zones colored in red have a significant illiteracy rate. In comparison, the mayoralties

Table 5. Number of reports per crime

Crime reported	Number of reports
Domestic violence	17995
Objects theft	14925
Nonviolent business theft	13428
Facts complain	11099
Fraud	10587
Threats	9933
Violent theft on a public road	6290

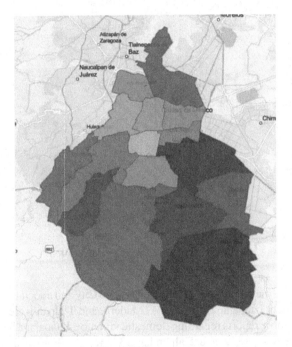

Fig. 6. Illiteracy rate

colored in yellow have a lower illiteracy rate. The illiteracy rate range is from 0.3 to 3.3%. At the same time, the crimes are represented as a heat map over the illiteracy rate

In order to retrieve another social indicator, Q5 was performed. In this query, the percentage of people with incomplete primary education. The results show that Milpa Alta, Iztapalapa, and La Magdalena Contreras are the three first mayoralties with a higher value, with 27.43%, 26.38%, and 25.33% respectively. In comparison, Benito Juárez is the mayoralty with the lowest percentage, which is 6.51%.

As the previous result related to social indicators with crime data, this table was transformed into a map layer, which is shown in Fig. 7.

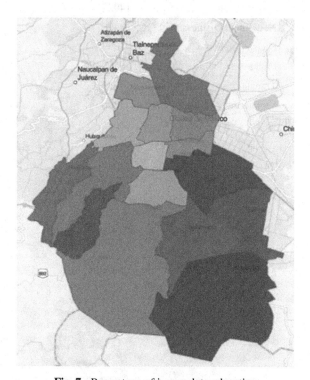

Fig. 7. Percentage of incomplete education

In order to relate the crime most reported in Mexico City and a social indicator Q6 was performed. In which, Iztapalapa, Gustavo A. Madero, and Tlalpan were retrieved as the mayoralties with more reports regarding domestic violence. Iztapalapa has 3837 reports; Gustavo A. Madero has 1879, and Tlalpan has 1372 reports. For these mayoralties, the illiteracy rate and domestic violence were retrieved. The illiteracy rate in Iztapapa is 2.37, in the second mayoralty is 1.76 and 1.84 for the third one. That result shows that the illiteracy rate is related to domestic violence. With an illiteracy rate of over 1.7%, these mayoralties have the highest numbers of domestic violence. Figure 8 shows the resulting map.

Performing Q7, the mayoralties with mayor illiteracy rates, and the number of domestic violence reports were retrieved. The mayoralties retrieved were Milpa Alta with

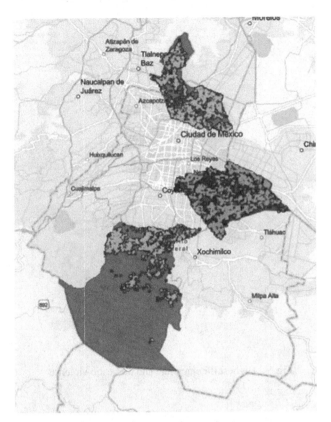

Fig. 8. Domestic violence and illiteracy rate

3.31%, Iztapalapa, which was already considered, Xochimilco with 2.28, and La Magdalena Contreras with 2.13%. Besides the number of domestic violence reports where the results show that Milpa Alta has 228, reports, Xochimilco 875, and La Magdalena Contreras 603. Compared to the previous result, the reports are not similar. However, in these mayoralties, there are fewer reports than in the previous result, and in these mayoralties the crime with the highest number of reports is domestic violence. The result was transformed, as previous results, into a map layer, shown in Fig. 9.

In order to compare the results, the Q8 query was performed. With this query, the three mayoralties with the lowest illiteracy rate were retrieved. The results show that Benito Juárez has 0.29%, Cuauhtemoc has 0.86%, and Miguel Hidalgo mayoralty has 1.09%. Besides, the domestic violence reports were retrieved, and the order in crime sorting according to the number of reports. In the three mayoralties mentioned is the fifth crime with more reports. Moreover, the number of domestic violence reports is 715 in Benito Juárez, 1489 in Cuauhtemoc, and 599 in Miguel Hidalgo. The results retrieved were transformed into a map layer shown in Fig. 10.

Even if domestic violence is the fifth crime reported in these mayoralties, the distribution in the heat map looks denser. The reason is that the number of crimes reported

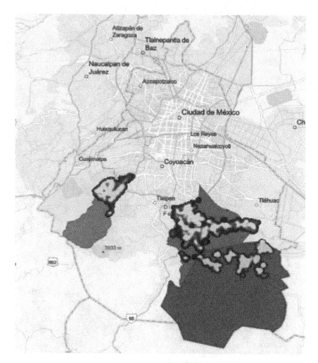

Fig. 9. Highest illiteracy rate and domestic violence

in the mayoralties shown in Fig. 10 is higher than the mayoralties mentioned in Q6 and Q7. Also, the urban zone is more significant in the mayoralties shown in Fig. 10.

According to results retrieved in Q6, Q7, and Q8, the illiteracy rate of over 1.7% can be considered a pattern in the domestic violence report. Performing more queries in data, in order to relate more social indicators with domestic violence in the areas mentioned, it will be possible to find other relations and consider them as patterns in the reporting of this crime. And not only with domestic violence, but with the other 26 crimes mentioned.

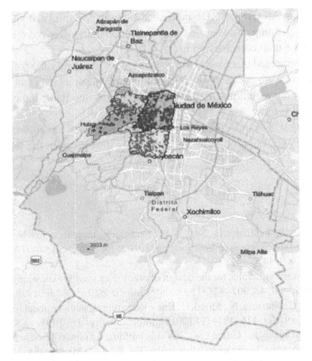

Fig. 10. Lowest illiteracy rates and domestic violence

5   Conclusions and Future Work

The presented work consisted of ontology development and an RDF generation to describe the crime reports in Mexico City and relate those reports with socioeconomic data from the area where the crimes occurred.

We presented the probable relations between the socioeconomic data and the crime reports. It was seen that some crimes have relations with some social variables, like relations between the illiteracy rate or the percentage of people with incomplete primary education with the number of crimes reported in an area. However, it is needed to make a probabilistic study to see if there is a correlation between the variables.

As future work, there will be added into the dataset new tuples using social networks extractions. Entity extraction will be made with natural language processing techniques.

Also, it will be considered new data about social indicators, is looking to add new about mobility and socioeconomic level from the mayoralties in the city. Once added, the correlation of these indicators with the crime reports will be calculated to decide the possible relevance of the study case indicators.

Although, as mentioned, the entities extracted can be added to the dataset of crime reports, and this dataset will be described in a new RDF using the ontology, which also could be enriched. However, another possibility is, once the RDF is published can be used queries to add new data to this knowledge representation model.

Instead of using ArcGIS, an RDF publisher with the possibility of visualization will be used to obtain the map at the same time. This publisher will avoid the data retrieved exportation and the map construction in ArcGIS.

It can be implemented machine learning techniques to identify the patterns and make the classification of each crime. In the part of the pattern, social data can be considered.

Machine learning techniques to identify the patterns and make the classification of each crime.

Also, this work will be published following the principles of linked data where anyone can access the SPARQL endpoint of the triple store developed in the RDF description of this dataset.

References

1. Pirnay-Dummer, P., Ifenthaler, D., Seel, N.M.: Knowledge representation. In: Seel, N.M. (ed.) Encyclopedia of the Sciences of Learning, pp. 101–211. Springer, Boston (2012). https://doi.org/10.1007/978-1-4419-1428-6
2. Gruber, T.: Toward principles for the design of ontologies used for knowledge sharing. Int. J. Hum. Comput. Stud. **43**, 907–928 (1993). https://doi.org/10.1006/ijhc.1995.1081
3. Jalil, M., Ling, C., Maizura, N., Mohd, F.: Knowledge representation model for crime analysis. Procedia Comput. Sci. **116**, 484–491 (2017). https://doi.org/10.1016/j.procs.2017.10
4. Thilagam, P., Srinivas, K.: Crime base: towards building a knowledge base for crime entities and their relationships from online newspapers. Inf. Process. Manage. **56** (2019). https://doi.org/10.1016/j.ipm.2019.102059
5. Kalemi, E., Domnori, E.: SMONT: an ontology for crime solving through social media. Int. J. Metadata Semant. Ontol. **12**, 71–81 (2019)
6. Acharya, G., Shakya, A.: Crime ontology extraction from news and social media. In: ICAEIC-2019, vol. 2, no. 1, Department of Electronics and Computer Engineering (2019)
7. Carnaz, G., Nogueira, V.B., Antunes, M.: Knowledge representation of crime-related events: a preliminary approach, Department of informatics, university of Évora, Portugal (2019)
8. Elezaj, O., Yayilgan, S.Y., Kalemi, E., Wendelberg, L., Abomhara, M., Ahmed, J.: Towards designing a knowledge graph-based framework for investigating and preventing crime on online social networks. In: Katsikas, S., Zorkadis, V. (eds.) e-Democracy 2019. CCIS, vol. 1111, pp. 181–195. Springer, Cham (2020). https://doi.org/10.1007/978-3-030-37545-4_12
9. Reyes-Ortiz, J.A.: Criminal event ontology population and enrichment using patterns recognition from text. Int. J. Pattern Recogn. Artif. Intell. **33**(11) (2019). https://doi.org/10.1142/s0218001419400147
10. Rahma, F., et al.: Analysis and implementation of ontology based text classification on criminality digital news IOP Conf. Ser. Mater. Sci. Eng. **662**, 022135 (2019). https://doi.org/10.1088/1757-899x/662/2/022135
11. Ko, G.-W., Kim, S.-W., Park, S.-J., No, Y.-J., Choi, S.-P.: Implementation of ontology-based service by exploiting massive crime investigation records: focusing on intrusion theft. J. Korean Soc. Libr. Inf. Sci. **53**(1), 57–81 (2019). https://doi.org/10.4275/KSLIS.2019.53.1.057
12. Endel, F., Piringer, H.: Data wrangling: making data useful again. IFAC-PapersOnLines **48**, 111–112 (2015)
13. Suárez-Figueroa, M., Gómez-Pérez, A., Motta, E., Gangemi, A.: Ontology Engineering in A Networked World. Springer, Berlin (2014). https://doi.org/10.1007/978-3-642-24794-1
14. Zou, L.: SPARQL. In: Liu, L., Özsu, M.T. (eds.) Encyclopedia of Database Systems. Springer, New York (2018). https://doi.org/10.1007/978-1-4614-8265-9

Crowdsourcing for *Sargassum* Monitoring Along the Beaches in Quintana Roo

Javier Arellano-Verdejo[1](✉) and Hugo E. Lazcano-Hernandez[2]

[1] El Colegio de la Frontera Sur, Chetumal, Quintana Roo, Mexico
javier.arellano@ecosur.mx
[2] Cátedras CONACYT-El Colegio de la Frontera Sur,
Chetumal, Quintana Roo, Mexico
hlazcanoh@ecosur.mx

Abstract. In recent years, the unusual arrival of *Sargassum* to the coasts of the Caribbean Sea has caused considerable damage, both economic and ecological. The monitoring of this macroalgae is a major challenge for researchers. Historically, satellite remote-sensing has been used for this purpose; however, limitations in the temporal and spatial resolution of available satellite platforms do not allow for the monitoring of *Sargassum* on beach coastlines. The increase in the capacity of communication and the decrease in the costs of technology have enhanced users' access to intelligent mobile devices. Crowdsourcing has proven to be successful in combining informational technology with a collaborative solution to complex problems. This study demonstrates how crowdsourcing and the new technologies, can be used to monitor *Sargassum* on the beaches in Quintana Roo, complementing satellite monitoring.

Keywords: Citizen science · Learning from crowds · Observing network · Coordinated observing system

1 Introduction

Sargassum belongs to the group of brown algae Phaeophyta that inhabit the seas around the world. The pelagic *Sargassum* subgroup, that is, the one that floats freely in the ocean, is composed of two species: *S. natans* and *S. fluitans*, the former being the most abundant in the Atlantic ocean. These species, belonging to the Phaeophyta Division, are typically pale brown-yellowish in color and can measure between 20 and 80 cm in diameter [1]. They have numerous nematocysts, which are small vesicles less than 1 cm in diameter that can float because of their gas composition [2]. Under optimal conditions of light, temperature, and salinity, *Sargassum* can double its mass in only 10 days, especially *S. fluitans* [3]. The recent arrival of *Sargassum* from 2018 to date on the Atlantic coast has quickly become both an environmental and a socio-economical challenge, with multi-factorial causes and leading to several unanswered questions.

Remote-sensing through satellite sensors is considered a powerful tool, it has demonstrated to have been important for Earth observation, and it has

© Springer Nature Switzerland AG 2020
M. F. Mata-Rivera et al. (Eds.): GIS LATAM 2020, CCIS 1276, pp. 49–62, 2020.
https://doi.org/10.1007/978-3-030-59872-3_4

traditionally been the main technique for observing *Sargassum* in the ocean [4]. *Sargassum* monitoring using satellite imagery has been possible for more than a decade, with the implementation of pelagic algae detection algorithms using a wide range of sensors. Some of these algorithms include: Maximum Chlorophyll Index (MCI) [4], MODIS Red Edge (MRE) [5], Index of floating algae (FAI) [6], alternative floating algae index (AFAI) [7] and ERISNet [8]. Most of these algorithms have essentially been used with low or moderate spatial resolution images (larger pixel size at 1 km). This allows for covering more extensive areas in one image and monitoring them more frequently. More detailed spatial scales have also been used, for example, the Landsat-8 [9] or Sentinel-2 [10]. However, the main disadvantage of these data can be found in the temporal resolution; for instance, the Landsat-8 provides an image of the same site each 16 days, which does not allow a daily monitoring. These approaches are limited by inputs, as some sensors may work well in oceanic environments, yet become saturated in coastal environments.

Due to technical limitations, some natural phenomena – such as *Sargassum* blooms – cannot be studied in detail through the use of traditional remote-sensing techniques. *Sargassum* observation along the beach requires daily images with a spatial resolution of less than one-meter. Nonetheless, the features of open source data satellite platforms do not allow accurate monitoring of *Sargassum* along the beaches. Table 1 shows a summary of the spatial and temporal resolution of four of the most important earth observation platforms which offer open source data: Landsat-8[1], through the sensors Operational Land Imager (OLI) and Thermal Infrared Sensor (TIRS); Sentinel-2,[2] through the sensor Multi Spectral Instrument (MSI); and Aqua and Terra,[3] through the sensor Moderate Resolution Imaging Spectroradiometer (MODIS) . Other satellite platforms offer imagery with accurate resolutions, but in most cases, they are not appropriate (i.e., they only offer low temporal resolution or they are not affordable). Due to the natural environment of the Caribbean Sea, the presence of clouds does not allow the optical satellite sensors to receive sufficient information. This causes several reactions, including: a) a drastic decrease in the amount of information available for monitoring the *Sargassum*, b) a challenge for conducting observations over extended periods of time (e.g., during rainy and/or hurricane season); and c) zero visibility of the Earth's surface resulting in the generation of false positives in most of the algorithms known in the literature.

2   State of the Art

The term crowdsourcing was coined by Howe et al., in 2006, to describe "the act of taking a job traditionally performed by a designated agent (usually an employee) and outsourcing it to an undefined, generally large group of people in the form of an open call" [11]. Crowdsourcing has been successfully applied in

---

[1] https://www.usgs.gov/land-resources/nli/landsat.

[2] https://sentinel.esa.int/web/sentinel/home.

[3] https://modis.gsfc.nasa.gov/about/specifications.php.

Table 1. Summary of the spatial and temporal resolution of four of the most important earth observation platforms which offering open-data: Sentinel-2, Landsat-8 and Aqua-Terra

Satellite platform	Sensor	Resolution	
		Time [days]	Spatial [m]
Sentinel 2	MSI	10 single 5 both	10, 20 & 60
Landsat 8	OLI & TIRS	16	15, 30 & 100
Aqua Terra	MODIS	1 or 2	250, 500 & 1000

numerous areas, including: Image Classification (CellSlider, Galaxy Zoo, Phylo, MOLT, Polyp Classification for Colon Cancer Detection), Character Recognition (ReCAPTCHA), Genome Annotation, Document Translation (DuoLingo), Protein Folding, RNA Structure Design (Foldit, EteRNA), and Algorithm Development (DTRA) [12]. Meteor Counter[4] is a platform launched by NASA for individual citizens to observe meteors. Creek Watch[5] was developed by IBM for monitoring and managing water resources. SciSpy[6] allows users to take screenshots of the plants and animals that are found. Finally, Greenappsandweb[7] is a platform that includes various applications for individual citizens with diverse objectives.

Another highly successful application related to ecology and biodiversity monitoring is iNaturalis, a citizen science project and online social network of naturalists, scientists, and biologists. This application maps and exchanges biodiversity observations around the world. One of the main features of this platform is that the information obtained can be widely accessed and is opensource data [13]. Epicollect, managed by the Big Data Institute of the University of Oxford, is a very robust platform in which, in addition to images, different data can be captured in text format through its user interface. It is designed for an expert user (e.g., scientists, technicians, and students), so it becomes complex for someone who is not familiarized with the topic [14].

In terms of *Sargassum* monitoring, the Marine Macroalgae Research lab at Florida International University (MMRL-FIU) is studying the occurrences of washed-up *Sargassum* landings on South Florida and Caribbean coastal areas, through the project "*Sargassum* Watch". This project is powered by the iNaturalist platform [15]. In early 2020, the *Sargassum* Watch project has 980 observations that have been carried out by 577 people. It contains mostly images related to the object of study since the intention is to taxonomically identify the image in each snapshot; however, there are also panoramic photographs. Additionally, MMRL-FIU linked the "*Sargassum* Watch" project to the "Epicollect" platform. The use of Epicollect allows for downloading the data and metadata

---

[4] http://ww17.meteorcounter.com.
[5] http://creekwatch.researchlabs.ibm.com.
[6] http://www.sciencechannel.com.
[7] https://www.greenappsandweb.com.

in different formats, enabling the interested community direct access to all of the information available. To date, there are 1,367 photographs in Epicollect [16]. On the other hand, in Mexico, the "National Commission for the Knowledge and Use of Biodiversity" (CONABIO)[8] manages the project "Monitoring pelagic *Sargassum* in the Mexican Atlantic" on the "Naturalista" platform. In early 2020, CONABIO's project has 154 observations which have been carried out by 50 people. Photographs include both close up and panoramic shots of *Sargassum*.

Several studies have demonstrated that crowdsourcing is a useful methodology for collecting and managing data. In the following section, this paper explains how the use of a novel crowdsourcing platform allowed for monitoring *Sargassum* on the beaches in the state of Quintana Roo.

3 Crowdsourcing for Monitoring *Sargassum* Along the Beaches in Quintana Roo

A pilot test was carried out in order to answer the question "Is crowdsourcing a useful technique to monitor *Sargassum* on the coast of Quintana Roo?" This pilot test consisted of creating and testing an infrastructure capable of collecting, processing, and distributing information related to the topic of the study. The platform was tested by dozens of users who participated voluntarily during the testing phase.

In short, the platform created is divided into two components: first, a mobile App that allows users to collect and send information regarding the *Sargassum* on the beaches; second, a central server that concentrates, analyses, and distributes the information collected by the users. In order to create the mobile application, we used the Java programming language and the Android operating system. For the implementation of the platform, we used Google Firebase. To analyze the data, we used the Python programming language with some libraries (e.g., pandas and scikit-learn). Finally, ESRI ArcGIS Online was used for the visualization and creation of the maps.

The process of monitoring *Sargassum* on the beaches in Quintana Roo through the use of crowdsourcing is shown in Fig. 1. The different stages included: data collection, data preprocessing, product generation to support decision making, data visualization and distribution of results as open source data to encourage other researchers to collaborate and extend the scope of the results obtained. The following sections demonstrate how crowdsourcing was used to improve the monitoring of the presence/absence, accumulation, and distribution of *Sargassum* on the beaches in Quintana Roo, complementing the classical satellite remote-sensing techniques currently employed.

---

[8] https://www.naturalista.mx/projects/monitoreo-de-sargazo-pelagico-en-el-atlantico-mexicano.

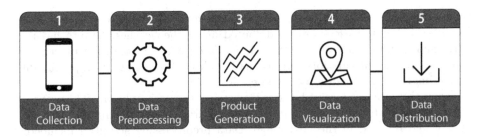

Fig. 1. Data flow of the monitoring process

The first stage in the process of monitoring was the collection of the data. To obtain the data, we developed a mobile application that allowed users to gather information about the condition of the beaches and upload the data to the platform on the cloud. The data collected included: medium-resolution photos (see Fig. 2), time, date, and geographic coordinates that allowed for determining the exact location of each photograph.

Fig. 2. Geo-located images collected by the users of Mahahual (Quintana Roo, Mexico) from September 14 and 15, 2019.

Since we wanted the system to be adopted by as many users as possible, the proposed model did not require users to have previous experience in monitoring the beaches. Higher volumes of information collected and uploaded by users of the platform resulted in an increased accuracy of the system. Based on the hypothesis that the users were distributed along the beaches, despite having little information, the system was able to determine the condition of nearby areas where the information was originally collected, creating an approximate global image of the condition of the beaches.

Once the data was received, the second step of the process began. The preprocessing stage included all of the necessary preparation for building the data-set that would be used in the next stage. Data preprocessing activities included: data cleansing (i.e., dealing with missing or invalid values, removing duplicates, and formatting appropriately); combining data from multiple sources (e.g., files, tables, platforms); and transforming the data into more useful variables. During this stage, images were also analyzed and classified into two groups: images with and without the presence of *Sargassum*. Furthermore, images with elements that are unrelated to the interest of this study were discarded. When all of the images were classified and the data was prepared, everything was stored in a geospatial database for the product generation.

In order to classify the set of data properly in two groups (i.e., images with the presence of sargassum and images without the presence of this macro-algae), the following strategies were used. First, the original set of images was classified by an expert into the two groups mentioned previously. Then, the new data set was again divided, forming two subsets: a training dataset (80%) and a validation dataset (20%).

Using the knowledge transfer technique, a pre-trained AlexNet neural network (for the ImageNet dataset) was employed. In order to fulfill the purposes of this study, we adapted the network by modifying the last layer. This made the classification of the two groups possible (e.g., presence and absence of sargassum). The technique of augmented data was used due to the small and unbalanced set of images obtained. Additionally, the K-Fold cross-validation test was used to improve and give certainty to the results.

Through Google Colab, Python programming language and the PyTorch library, a GPU was used to perform a 10-hour training process for 1000 epochs. The results demonstrated an accuracy of more than 90%. Considering the data set available, we consider this to be a good result. As part of our future work, we will continue to improve the process of generalizing the network using the images that become available.

Figure 3 shows some examples of images with the presence of *Sargassum*. A great diversity of elements can be observed in each of the photographs (e.g., *Sargassum*, garbage, sand, water, clouds, boats, piers, buildings, and palm trees). In addition, it is possible to see multiple differences between the photographs (i.e., illumination, color, angle, light, type of close-up, and camera position). This represented a big challenge for automatic classification.

At the end of the data preprocessing stage, the information was analyzed, resulting in a set of tools that can be used to inform the condition of the beaches in near real-time. This benefits the population, especially visitors who use the

Fig. 3. Some examples of the different types of photographs and the wide diversity of elements in the images obtained through Crowdsourcing.

beaches as recreation and rest areas. Additionally, these tools can serve as support for local authorities responsible for cleaning and conserving the beaches.

As part of the products that are currently being generated in the third step of the process, the following are included:

– Definition of areas with and without the presence of *Sargassum*.
– Creation of heat maps that indicate user activity.
– Analysis of time series to study the behavior of the platform.
– Design of reports that examine the state of the various beaches for which information is available.

The visualization of the collected data is a fundamental step during the monitoring process since it enabled us to observe and identify the current condition of the beaches. Furthermore, it served to identify possible distribution patterns of the accumulated *Sargassum* in defined time intervals. This could be fundamental for the planning and preparation stages before the arrival of these macroalgae.

The use of maps for visualizing the data was indispensable. As shown in Fig. 4, the geolocation of the points on the map allowed for conducting studies using geographic information system tools (e.g., heat maps). In the case of heat zones, each one highlights the areas or beaches with the most activity by users. More data allowed the monitoring system to be more robust from a statistical point of view. The status of the areas that had higher activity allowed to infer the status of nearby areas with high precision, even when there was not sufficient information from such zones directly.

Other methods of visualization of the information included different types of charts and graphs (e.g., pie, bars, and lines). These visual representations helped summarize the data collected in an executive way. Some examples included the

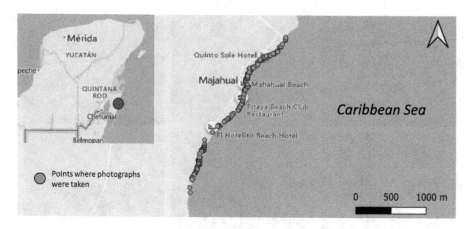

Fig. 4. Data points collected for Mahahual beach.

total points per zone, the zones with more photos that report *Sargassum*, the progression of activity by users over time, among others (see Fig. 5).

It is important to highlight that the proposed system was not only in charge of monitoring the areas with the presence of *Sargassum*. It also highlighted the areas that did not have the presence of this macroalgae. This is useful for tourists because it allows them to make decisions about which beaches they should or should not visit. With a correct classification of the images, the proposed system can automatically generate a status (e.g., green, yellow, red) that indicates the areas that are ideal for their visit and those areas where the authorities should focus their efforts to carry out the cleaning process.

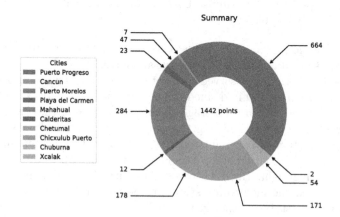

Fig. 5. Point per zone report

The final step in this process was related to data distribution. Due to the origin of the data as well as the impact that the results can have for further research related to the monitoring of *Sargassum*, it is necessary to distribute the data obtained permanently and transparently in the open source data model. The publication of information as Open Source Data is an increasingly common practice that aims to make certain types of data freely available to everyone, without restrictions of copyright, patent, or other control mechanisms. Open source data can come from any source, such as scientific results, governments, private companies, and others.

One of the main reasons why more and more organizations are publishing their data is due to interoperability, which denotes the ability of diverse systems and organizations to work together. In our case, interoperability was defined as the ability to integrate different data-sets for the study of the accumulation, distribution, and behavior of *Sargassum* on the beaches in Quintana Roo. This ability to integrate components is essential for building complex systems. Without interoperability, it is almost impossible to achieve - as demonstrated by the famous myth of the "Babel Tower" where the inability to communicate resulted in the collapse of the entire effort to build the tower.

4   Results

In order to evaluate the sustainability of using crowdsourcing as a method for collecting data related to the presence and absence of *Sargassum* on the beaches in Quintana Roo, the application we designed was distributed and tested with a total of 32 citizens who voluntarily obtained images of the most frequently visited beaches in Quintana Roo. Table 2 shows a list of the beaches and the number of photos obtained.

Table 2. Number of photos obtained for the Quintana Roo state beaches

Location	Data points
Mahahual	**284**
Chetumal	178
Puerto Morelos	47
Playa del Carmen	23
Calderitas	12
Cancún	7
Xcalak	2

At the same time, the same activity was also carried out, with a total of 16 people, in some beaches in the state of Yucatán. The results are shown in Table 3.

The period during which the piloting was carried out took place between July 1, 2019 and October 31, 2019. At the end of the piloting phase, 1442 photos were

Table 3. Number of photos obtained for the Yucatán state beaches

Location	Data points
Puerto Progreso	**664**
Chicxulub Puerto	171
Chuburna	54

obtained from the states of Quintana Roo and Yucatán in Mexico, by a total of 48 participants.

As demonstrated in Fig. 6, at the beginning of the piloting phase, the activity uploaded by participants was very low, almost null. The number of photos during the first month was zero. This could be due to a number of reasons, including the lack of knowledge on how to the use the application, or the lack of awareness on behalf of the participants about the relevance of their participation for monitoring *Sargassum* on the beaches.

Beginning in the second month of the study, a progressive increase in the activity can be observed, which implies an increasingly active participation by the community. Figure 6 shows that, at least for this study, the processes involving crowdsourcing require a minimum time before they are adopted. Thus, this type of projects are not adopted immediately, which leads to very interesting conclusions regarding the minimum average time that must be considered before the information from individuals starts to flow continuously.

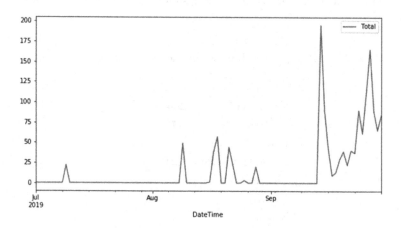

Fig. 6. Application activity

To exemplify the advantages of Crowdsourcing, we can visualize that we are interested in knowing the beach conditions of Mahahual for September 15, 2019. Around that date, the Landsat platform offers two scenes, one for September 9 and 25 (Landsat-8 imagery courtesy of the U.S. Geological Survey). On the other hand, the Sentinel-2 platform offers us 5 scenes: September 9, 12, 14, 24, and 29 (Sentinel-2 imagery courtesy of the European Space Agency). The scene closest to the desired date is that of September 14 from the Sentinel 2 platform; however, due to weather conditions, it is only possible to observe a cloud over the city of Mahahual. The next closest date with images available is September 9. Figure 7 shows the scenes of the Landsat and Sentinel platforms corresponding to September 9, 2019. In Fig. 7a, the image of Landsat 8 is emphasized, and in Fig. 7c the image of Sentinel 2 is emphasized. In both figures, it is possible to appreciate the differences in spatial resolution between the two platforms. Figure 7b is a close-up of the Landsat-8 image with pixels of 30 m per side. Figure 7d is a close-up of the Sentinel-2 image with pixels of 20 m per side. In Figs. 7b and 7d, it is possible to observe that the pixels corresponding to the beach mostly present information on both land and water, so they are not a reliable input to be used in the different algorithms for monitoring *Sargassum* and generally do not offer reliability for any type of analysis.

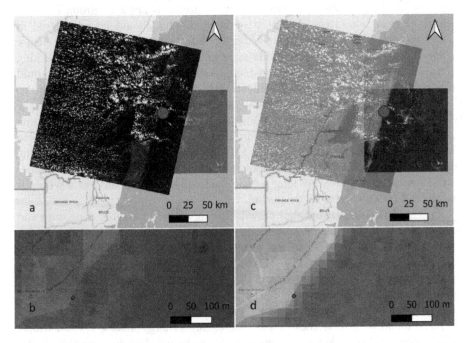

Fig. 7. RGB imagery from the south of Quintana Roo, Mexico, a) Landsat-8, b) Landsat-8 Close-up, c) Sentinel-2, d) Close-up Sentinel-2.

As a summary, there was no information from remote sensors. However, with crowdsourcing, we were able to obtain the imagery to carry out the *Sargassum* monitoring. This exercise exemplifies how, in some cases, the participation of citizens from the community contributes to satellite information and has the potential to become an alternative source of data.

5   Conclusions

The present study demonstrated the sustainability of crowdsourcing as a method that can be useful for monitoring the presence or absence of Sargassum along the beaches in Quintana Roo. However, there are challenges that must be addressed to guarantee the possibility of continuing the monitoring over an extended period of time, which could be months or years. This study found both advantages and challenges to crowdsourcing. In the present study 1142 photographs were uploaded to the platform, from 10 different cities distributed along two states of the Yucatan peninsula, without incurring in any logistical expenses. The pictures obtained allowed for monitoring the beaches. On the other hand, we encountered several challenges as well. Crowdsourcing is well accepted by small ecology-sensitive organizations (e.g., turtle protection groups), as well as by scholars and institutions interested in coastal ecosystems. Nevertheless, the participation of society, in general, was very low despite the dissemination carried out through conferences in different institutions and social networks. We consider that this low participation is because crowdsourcing is not a common habit in society, at least not in the southeast of Mexico. This should be considered in further research when using this method for data collection. In order to ensure higher success rates when using this type of methods, we suggest networking with social sciences experts. Another technological challenge we faced and could be improved is the automatic classification of images. As a positive feature to the study area, in the past few years, the tourism industry has increased the telecommunication infrastructure along the coastline of the state of Quintana Roo, mainly in the northern area, including Benito Juarez, Isla Mujeres, Puerto Morelos, and Solidaridad. Therefore, this study considers that crowdsourcing could be a powerful method to support Sargassum monitoring along the beaches in this geographical area, as long as the participation of society as a whole is guaranteed for the entire study period.

This study demonstrated that crowdsourcing allowed for generating data and information that did not exist previously. This method is potentially useful for other researchers. However, we suggest that for this type of tool to be considered more advantageous, it is necessary for large numbers of people to adopt it and participate in a coordinated way during the different stages of the process. Crowdsourcing brings together society, researchers, industries, and the government, all working collectively for the benefit of the environment. One strategy we recommend to involve more users, is creating synergy among organizations, associations, and companies that coexist along the beaches; for example, turtle protection groups, garbage-monitoring teams, hoteliers, and government institutions are all focused on preserving the beaches along the coasts and could benefit crowdsourcing tremendously.

6   Future Work

The main objective of this study was to show if the use of crowdsourcing could support the monitoring of Sargassum along the beaches in Quintana Roo by complementing traditional satellite remote sensing techniques. Many aspects of this study can be improved (e.g., increasing the neural network accuracy, enhancing the web and mobile platforms, and/or extending the number of users). However, one of the most important aspects that has not yet been achieved, is ensuring the sets of images collected through the platform are available for all the interested parties (researchers and community in general). As part of our future research, we must focus on resolving the legal and logistical aspects related to this matter, so that the information can be accessed freely without incurring in copyright problems.

Acknowledgement. We thank the U.S. Geological Survey (USGS) and the European Space Agency (ESA) for the courtesy of providing the Landsat-8 and Sentinel-2 imagery used in this study. Additionally, we would like to thank Deon Victoria Heffington for her help in the revisions and edition of this manuscript.

References

1. Uribe-Martínez, A., Guzmán-Ramírez, A., Arreguín-Sánchez, F., Cuevas, E.: El sargazo en el Caribe mexicano, revisión de una historia impensable. Gobernanza y Manejo de las Costas y Mares ante la Incertidumbre, p. 743 (2020)
2. South Atlantic Fishery Management Council. Fishery Management Plan for Pelagic Sargassum Habitat of the South Atlantic Region, South Carolina, 183 pp. (2002)
3. Hanisak, M.D., Samuel, M.A.: Growth rates in culture of several species of Sargassum from Florida, USA. In: Twelfth International Seaweed Symposium, pp. 399–404. Springer, Dordrecht (1987). https://doi.org/10.1007/978-94-009-4057-4_59
4. Gower, J., Hu, C., Borstad, G., King, S.: Ocean color satellites show extensive lines of floating Sargassum in the Gulf of Mexico. IEEE Trans. Geosci. Remote **44**(12), 3619–25 (2006). https://doi.org/10.1109/TGRS.2006.882258
5. Gower, J., Young, E., King, S.: Satellite images suggest a new Sargassum source region in 2011. Remote Sens. Lett. **4**(8), 764–73 (2013). https://doi.org/10.1080/2150704X.2013.796433
6. Hu, C.: A novel ocean color index to detect floating algae in the global oceans. Remote Sens. Environ. **113**(10), 2118–29 (2009). https://doi.org/10.1016/j.rse.2009.05.012
7. Wang, M., Hu, C.: Mapping and quantifying Sargassum distribution and coverage in the Central West Atlantic using MODIS observations. Remote Sens. Environ. **183**, 350–67 (2016). https://doi.org/10.1016/j.rse.2016.04.019
8. Arellano-Verdejo, J., Lazcano-Hernandez, H.E., Cabanillas-Terán, N.: ERISNet: deep neural network for Sargassum detection along the coastline of the Mexican Caribbean. PeerJ. **7**, e6842 (2019). https://doi.org/10.7717/peerj.6842
9. Witherington, B., Hirama, S., Hardy, R.: Young sea turtles of the pelagic Sargassum-dominated drift community: habitat use, population density, and threats. Mar. Ecol. Progr. Ser. **463**, 1–22 (2012). https://doi.org/10.3354/meps09970
10. Cuevas, E., Uribe-Martínez, A., Liceaga-Correa, M.D.: A satellite remote-sensing multi-index approach to discriminate pelagic Sargassum in the waters of the Yucatan Peninsula, Mexico. Int. J. Remote Sens. **39**(11), 3608–3627 (2018). https://doi.org/10.1080/01431161.2018.1447162

11. Howe, J.: The rise of crowdsourcing. Wired Mag. **14**(6), 1–4 (2006)
12. Good, B.M., Su, A.I.: Crowdsourcing for bioinformatics. Bioinformatics **29**(16), 1925–1933 (2013)
13. iNaturalist Homepage. www.inaturalist.org. Accessed 26 May 2020
14. Epicollect Homepage. https://five.epicollect.net/. Accessed 26 May 2020
15. Sargassum watch project Homepage. https://colombia.inaturalist.org/projects/sargassum-watch-inaturalist-version. Accessed 28 May 2020
16. Epicollect Sargassum-watch project Homepage. https://five.epicollect.net/project/sargassum-watch/data. Accessed 28 May 2020

Air Quality and Its Relationship
with the Community Birds from the Sierra de
Guadalupe, México

Itzel Ibarra-Meza[1] ⓘ, Hugo Barrera-Huertas[2] ⓘ, and Eugenia López-López[3](✉) ⓘ

[1] Departamento de Ingeniería en Sistemas Ambientales, Escuela Nacional de Ciencias Biológicas, Maestría en Sostenibilidad e Innovación en Tecnología Ambiental, Instituto Politécnico Nacional, Av. Wilfrido Massieu 399, Unidad Profesional Adolfo López Mateos, Zacatenco, Col. Nueva Industrial Vallejo, 07738 Alcaldía Gustavo A. Madero, CDMX, Mexico
[2] Laboratorio de Sistemas de Información Geográfica, Departamento de Ingeniería en Sistemas Ambientales, Escuela Nacional de Ciencias Biológicas, Instituto Politécnico Nacional, Av. Wilfrido Massieu 399, Unidad Profesional Adolfo López Mateos, Zacatenco, Col. Nueva Industrial Vallejo, 07738 Alcaldía Gustavo A. Madero, CDMX, Mexico
hubarrera@ipn.mx
[3] Laboratorio de Evaluación de la Salud de los Ecosistemas Acuáticos, Departamento de Zoología, Escuela Nacional de Ciencias Biológicas, Instituto Politécnico Nacional, Prol. Carpio y Plan de Ayala s/n, Col. Sto. Tomás, 11340 Alcaldía Miguel Hidalgo, CDMX, Mexico
eulopez@ipn.mx

Abstract. The air quality in Mexico City (CDMX) is currently evaluated by the Air and Health Index (AHI), which does not consider the joint effect of the mixed pollutants, neither the damage to biodiversity. The development of an index that evaluates these effects and the use of atmospheric dispersion and trajectory models such as the Hybrid Single-Particle Lagrangian Integrated Trajectory Model (HYSPLIT) supports the design of an Integrated Air Quality Index (IAQI). This study aimed to evaluate the relationship between bird diversity and air quality, based on a pollutant analysis and the IAQI at the Sierra de Guadalupe, CDMX, Mexico (SG-CDMX). A bird census was conducted at SG-CDMX (Jan-Feb 2020). The values of structural and functional diversity of communities and AHI of CO, O_3, Particulate Matter (PM) $PM_{2.5}$ and PM_{10} were obtained. The relationship between bird diversity and the IAQI proposed was assessed with a Principal Component Analysis. The HYSPLIT model was computed using satellite images. Heat maps of AHI and weather parameters were developed with QGIS. Southern sector sites reached the highest IAQI and AHI values, which were associated with the higher vehicular influx and industrial activity (IAQI increased when air quality was lower). While the northern sites presented the highest values of structural diversity and air quality, these sites have conservation land use and lower anthropogenic activity. Furthermore, the HYSPLIT model shows that the trajectories and movement of particles are from southwest to northeast.

Keywords: Air Quality · Integrated Air Quality Index · Birds · HYSPLIT model · Sierra de Guadalupe

© Springer Nature Switzerland AG 2020
M. F. Mata-Rivera et al. (Eds.): GIS LATAM 2020, CCIS 1276, pp. 63–79, 2020.
https://doi.org/10.1007/978-3-030-59872-3_5

1   Introduction

Mexico City has had several air pollution-related problems for more than 40 years. These problems are mainly due to the intense burning of fossil fuels, generated mainly by mobile (motor vehicles) and fixed (industry) sources, resulting in high levels of air pollution [1]. Sierra de Guadalupe Protected Natural Area is located in the north of Mexico City and the south of the State of Mexico, near to the Vallejo Industrial Area, in Gustavo A. Madero and Azcapotzalco mayors, and the industrial zone of the Tultitlán and Tlalnepantla municipalities [2]. This area is highly influenced by vehicular traffic and industrial emissions. It is known that the wind direction in Mexico City generally goes from the north to the south, which causes the pollutants of the area to be dragged towards the central and southern areas of Mexico City [3]. Thus, the northern part of the CDMX has become a place of great importance for the study and evaluation of air quality.

Associated with high levels of air pollution, various damages to human health have been observed and studied, which have been found mainly in the respiratory, circulatory, and cardiac systems [4]. However, damage to wildlife and ecosystems has also been observed, such as birds, which have exhibited damage at different levels of biological organization, from cellular to population [5, 6]. Birds have also been used as air quality bioindicators and as biological condition indicators of various ecosystems [7, 8].

Due to the high air pollution episodes in the Metropolitan Zone of the Valley of Mexico (MZVM), in 1982 the Metropolitan Index of Air Quality (IMECA) was developed, widely disseminated in 2006 [9]. However, since February 18, 2020, the Air Quality and Health Risk Index "Air and Health Index" (AHI) came into force, which was incorporated by the Official Mexican Standard NOM-172-SEMARNAT-2019, leaving IMECA deprecated. Both indexes address the different risks of each pollutant criteria in human health and established risk categories for the different sectors of the population. None of these takes into account the risk to human health from the mixture of all criteria pollutants since they are only assessed for each pollutant separately [10]. On the other hand, these indexes only refer to risks to human health and do not cover the risks or damage that may arise in biodiversity and ecosystems.

For this reason, it is important to develop an index to assess the damage exerted by the mixture of various pollutants to human health, biodiversity, and ecosystems. Likewise, the use of tools such as the Hybrid Single-Particle Lagrangian Integrated Trajectory Model (HYSPLIT) and the elaboration of heat maps with QGIS, allow us knowing where the atmospheric pollutants moves and its possible affectations [11]. Thus, they are also very useful in the development and interpretation of an Integrated Air Quality Index, as well as in any assessment of air quality.

2   Background and State-of-the-Art

2.1   Air Quality

In Mexico, since the 1950s, some air quality studies were already carried out, which considered some effects of air quality on human health. While, in the 1960s four atmospheric monitoring stations were installed to assess the air quality of the Metropolitan

Zone of the Valley of Mexico and in 1973 there were already 14, incorporating them into the United Nations Program [9]. Currently, there is the Atmospheric Monitoring System which has 45 monitoring stations located at different mayoralties of the CDMX and at some municipalities of the State of Mexico [12].

Since February 2020 the Air and Health Index is calculated, which is reported every hour on the website www.aire.cdmx.gob.mx, informing the population about the current air quality condition. This index entered into force due to the publication of NOM-172-SEMARNAT-2019. Also, this Air and Health Index displaced the Metropolitan Air Quality Index (IMECA), which was designed in 1982 and entered into force in 2006 [10].

In recent years, several authors have conducted various air quality assessments in Mexico City and other Mexican metropolitan areas. They have used the data obtained from different monitoring stations of the Metropolitan Zone of the Valley of Mexico. They have proposed various methods of information analysis, such as sorting models (Principal Component Analysis) [13]. They have also assessed the pollution levels at different times of the year [14] and have used satellites for monitoring urban CO emissions [15].

2.2 Birds as Bioindicators

Birds are considered good environmental and air quality indicators [16]; thus, several researchers have used them as indicators in various regions of the world. These researchers found a relationship between the high species diversity with green urban areas; as well as, associated with a good quality of life [17, 18]. Similarly, a relationship has been found between various damages from the individual level (in different organs and tissues), population level (reproductive), and community level, with the constant exposure to atmospheric pollutants [5, 6].

On the other hand, birds have been used to assess the biological condition of various ecosystems. Regional assessments of forests and the impact of different land uses have been carried out, through the relationship between functional diversity, structural diversity and environmental parameters that has a remarkable relationship with alterations in the ecosystem [7, 8, 19]. These studies have enabled researchers to detect early warning signals of the current condition of ecosystems and alert decision-makers implementing appropriate measures to protect and prevent ecosystem degradation.

To know the bird community, is important assessing the structural diversity (the diversity of organisms in the community) through the Simpson Index, Shannon Index, and Maximum Diversity. As well as which species are dominant or what is the evenness of the ecosystem [20]. Functional diversity is obtained to understand the relationship between structural diversity, community, and ecosystem functioning. In the case of birds, functional diversity can be known through food guilds, food substrate, habitat preference, and nesting mode, among other traits of birdlife or ecological histories, and the different environmental parameters assessed [8].

3   Objective

This work aimed to evaluate the relationship between the structural diversity scores form the Sierra de Guadalupe bird community and the air quality in the area, by analyzing air pollutants, using the HYSPLIT model and heat maps with QGIS; as well as integrating an index of pollutants to know the biological condition of the Sierra de Guadalupe.

4   Materials and Methods

4.1   Study Area

The study was carried out in the Sierra de Guadalupe, which is in the northern portion of Mexico City (CDMX) in Gustavo A. Madero mayor. It is between 2340 and 2980 meters above sea level (masl) and is considered a set of volcanic elevations formed in the Miocene [21]. Four study sites were selected, three within the Sierra de Guadalupe y la Armella Protected Natural Area (PNA) polygon and one outside the PNA, in an urban area (Fig. 1).

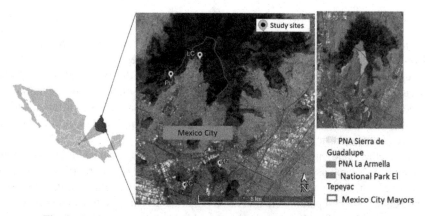

Fig. 1. Study area, Sierra de Guadalupe, CDMX, Mexico, and study sites

This area has not been completely studied, mainly in terms of air quality and the bird community. Sierra de Guadalupe is located in the northern part of Mexico City and is considered a relict natural site; however, it has been fragmented by settlements and various human activities, which place biological integrity and ecosystem services at risk [22]. Likewise, this site has been the refuge of a wide variety of resident and migratory bird species (96 species), as well as reptiles and flora, among other species [23]. Also, the PNA Management Plan Program notes that this site provides a variety of environmental services, such as CO_2 and suspended particles capture. These arguments lead to declaring this site (with particular biotic and abiotic characteristics) as a Protected Natural Area under the management category of Area Subject to Ecological Conservation.

The study sites La Caballeriza (LC) and El Panal (PL) are located within the PNA in the north, in these sites the predominant land use is conservation; however, there are urban settlements in the surrounding area [23]. On the other hand, the Site Zacatenco Module (MZ) is also located within the PNA polygon, on the hill of Zacatenco, on the side is the Mexico-Pachuca highway which has high vehicular traffic. Likewise, this site presents the use of conservation land and regular and irregular urban settlements (16). The Zacatenco Sports Zone (ZC) site is located outside the PNA polygon, in an urban area with urban and industrial settlements [24].

4.2 Birds Census

A bird census was conducted during the cold dry season (Jan-Feb 2020), at four study sites in the Sierra de Guadalupe, CDMX (MZ, LC, PL, and ZC). Three 30-meter-long transects were drawn at each study site, and birds that were seen or heard were recorded over a 10 min period, with the help of binoculars, cameras, and identification guides.

The survey was also conducted between 8 am and 11 am. The characteristics of the habitat (soil, understory, midstory, canopy, forest, forest shore, non-forest), the activity they were doing (singing, eating, flying, jumping between branches, etc.), food preference (insectivorous, granivore, frugivore, nectarivorous, carnivorous, omnivorous) and food stratum (foliage, soil, air, bark, water) were registered.

From a bibliographic review and the data recorded in the survey, a database was developed with the functional traits of each species.

4.3 Atmospheric Monitoring

Concentration data and AHI values of CO, O_3, $PM_{2.5}$, and PM_{10} were obtained from the atmospheric monitoring stations La Presa (LPR), Xalostoc (XAL), Gustavo A. Madero (GAM), Camarones (CAM), Tultitlán (TLI), and Tlalnepantla (TLA) of the Metropolitan Area of the Valley of Mexico and weather parameters (Relative Humidity, Wind Direction, Wind Speed, Air Temperature) using a portable weather station (DAVIS VantagePro) and an automatic weather station of the National Weather System.

4.4 Birds Community Structural and Functional Diversity

From the records of bird species, the values of species richness and abundance values were obtained, as well as Simpson diversity, Shannon diversity, maximum diversity, and evenness, with the following Eqs. (1, 2, 3 and 4).
Shannon diversity index

$$H' = \sum\nolimits_{i=1}^{s} p_i Log_2 p_i \tag{1}$$

Simpson diversity index

$$D = 1 - \sum\nolimits_{i=1}^{s} \frac{1}{p_i} \tag{2}$$

Maximum diversity index

$$H_{max} = Ln(s) \tag{3}$$

Evenness index

$$J = \frac{H'}{Hmax} \tag{4}$$

Where:

- H_{max} = Sample information content (bits/individual)
- H' = Diversity Index
- s = Number of species
- pi = Ratio of the p_{esim} individuals of the species i with respect to the total individuals of the whole species in the community
- D = Probability that more organisms of the same species exist once the first has been collected
- J = Considers the H' diversity ratio of a place with respect to the maximum diversity that could be in that site
  Similarly, the functional diversity value of 25 functional trait metrics belonging to 7 categories of bird species life histories was obtained (Table 1).
  Functional diversity was assessed with the RAO coefficient from the following equation (Eq. 5):

$$FD = \sum_{i=1}^{s} \sum_{j=1}^{s} dij\, pi\, pj \tag{5}$$

Where:
FD = Functional divergence of food guilds
s = Number of species present in the community
pi and pj = Proportion of individuals of the species in the community
d_{ij} = Varies from 0 to 1.
Values close to 1 imply greater functional divergence or better use of the resources available in the environment; whereas, values close to 0 imply a greater overlap of niche in resource usage.

It was observed that data did not present normality neither homoscedasticity and significant differences between study sites were achieved through the non-parametric Kruskal-Wallis test.

4.5 Development of the Integrated Air Quality Index

The Integrated Air Quality Index (IAQI) was developed, based on an adaptation to the method of calculating the Integrated Biomarker Response [25]. This index was drawn up from the values of the AHI of CO, O_3, $PM_{2.5}$, and PM_{10} and the weather parameters of temperature, relative humidity, wind direction, and wind speed. The values were standardized with the next mathematical procedure [26]:

The average value from each parameter was obtained for each site (X) and the average value of each parameter for all study sites (m).

Table 1. Categories of selected functional traits

Class I	Habitat preference
Class II	Nesting
Class III	Food stratum
Class IV	Food guild
Class V	Sexual dimorphism
Class VI	Vulnerability value
Class VII	Residence category
Class VIII	Risk category
Class IX	Endemism category

The standard deviation value (s) of the average values of each study site (X) was obtained.

The value of Y was calculated with the next equation (Eq. 6):

$$Y = (X - m)/s \tag{6}$$

Z was obtained, where $Z = Y$ or $Z = -Y$, as appropriate.

To get the value of S (score), the minimum value of each of the parameters from all the study sites was firstly calculated and the absolute value of the study site was added to Z (Eq. 7):

$$S = Z + |Min| \tag{7}$$

The value of S was represented with a radial plot, where each vector represents one of the air quality parameters. The area of the triangle defined for two successive parameters, with k parameter values, was obtained with the following Eq. (8):

$$A_i = S_i \times S_{i+1} \times \sin\left(\frac{2\pi}{k}\right)/2 \tag{8}$$

Whereas, the value of IAQI was calculated with the following Eq. (9):

$$IAQI = \sum_{i=1}^{k} Ai \tag{9}$$

Where:

Ai = triangle area value

S = parameter score value

k = total number of parameters.

Higher index values indicate higher air pollution or poor air quality.

The relationship between the structural and functional diversity of bird community and IAQI was assessed by a Principal Component Analysis.

Besides, the HYSPLIT atmospheric transport and dispersion model of particles (including PM_{10} and $PM_{2.5}$) was made through IMO-NASA satellite imagery. On the other hand, heat maps were made with the AHI values of CO, O_3, $PM_{2.5}$, and PM_{10}, as well as with the parameters of temperature, relative humidity and wind speed with the QGIS software.

5 Results and Discussion

5.1 Birds Community

A total of 48 bird species were recorded at the four study sites during the January-February census. The highest species richness was observed at the MZ site and the lowest in PL. On the other hand, the ZC site presented the highest values of relative abundance, Simpson diversity, maximum diversity, and functional diversity; while Shannon's evenness and diversity were higher in PL.

The nesting category presented the highest FD values, while the risk category obtained the lowest value of FD.

5.2 Meteorological Parameters

The highest temperature was observed at the ZC site with mean values of 19.3 °C, in contrast, the MZ site had the lowest temperature values ($p \leq 0.05$) (Fig. 2). Also, the ZC site had the highest relative humidity percentage (61%) and the MZ site obtained the lowest relative humidity, no significant differences were found ($p \leq 0.05$) (Fig. 3). On the other hand, the highest wind speed was presented at the ZC site with 3.5 m/s and at the MZ site the lowest wind speed was presented, no significant differences were found ($p \geq 0.05$) (Fig. 4).

5.3 Air Quality

The highest values of CO, PM_{10}, and $PM_{2.5}$ were observed at the MZ site, while lower concentrations were observed at LC and PL sites. The AHI value of O_3 is the highest at the ZC site and the lowest values of this pollutant were presented in LC and PL. The highest IAS values of CO, PM_{10}, and $PM_{2.5}$ were observed at the MZ site, while lower concentrations were detected at LC and PL sites. The AHI value of O_3 was higher at the ZC site and the lowest values of the ZC pollutant were presented in LC and PL (Fig. 5, 6, 7, and 8).

The highest IAQI was presented at the ZC site, followed by MZ; while the best air quality was observed in LC (Fig. 9).

The HYSPLYT backward trajectories for particles (assuming PM_{10} and $PM_{2.5}$) occurs from southwest to northeast at 100 and 500 masl; and it is also possible to observe in Fig. 10, that particles at a higher altitude (1500–2000 m above the surface) comes from east showing pathways greater than trajectories at 100 and 500 masl.

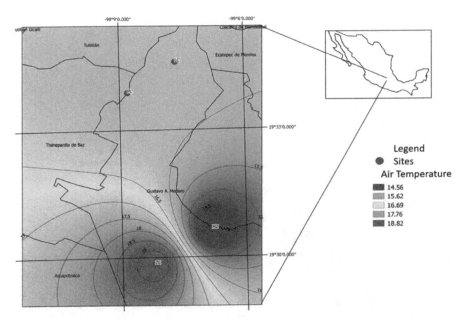

Fig. 2. Heat map for air temperature. Made with QGIS using Kriging technique.

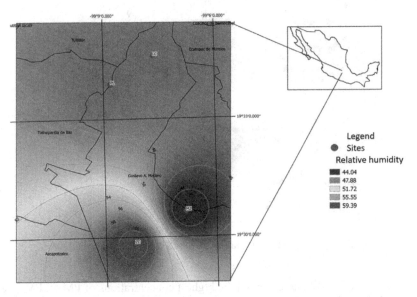

Fig. 3. Heat map for Relative Humidity. Made with QGIS using Kriging technique.

5.4 Principal Component Analysis

The biplot of the principal component analyses showed that the ZC site presented the highest values of temperature, relative humidity, air speed, IAQI, O_3, AHI, and functional

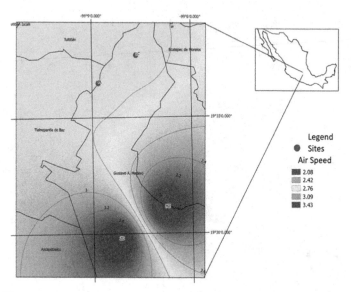

Fig. 4. Heat map for air speed. Made with QGIS using Kriging technique.

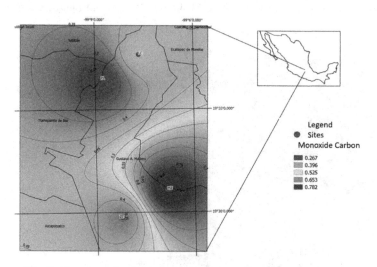

Fig. 5. Heat-maps for CO. Made with QGIS using Kriging technique.

diversity. While, the MZ site observed the highest concentrations of $PM_{2.5}$, PM_{10}, and CO, as well as the highest values of species abundance and specific richness. On the other hand, PL and LC sites had the highest air quality values, i.e. the lowest IAQI and AHI values (Fig. 11).

It is important to note that the ZC and MZ sites are located in the southern portion of the Sierra de Guadalupe and are the closest study sites to the urban area of the CDMX. The ZC site is located in an area with urban land use and industrial activity [24] but with

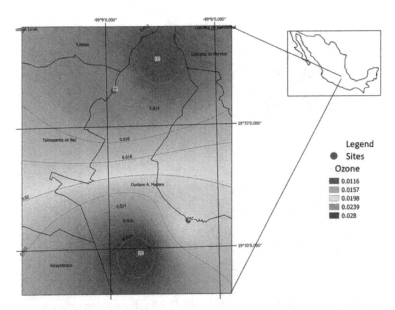

Fig. 6. Heat-maps for O₃. Made with QGIS using Kriging technique.

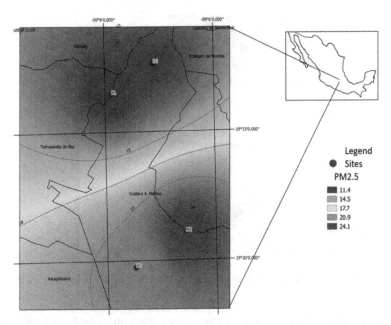

Fig. 7. Heat-maps for PM₂.₅. Made with QGIS using Kriging technique.

large green areas, allowing the settlement of birds. On the other hand, the MZ site is part of the PNA Sierra de Guadalupe/La Armella, which has a land use of conservation;

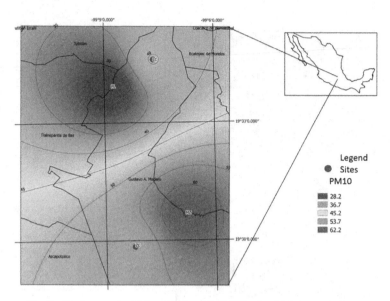

Fig. 8. Heat-maps for PM_{10}. Made with QGIS using Kriging technique.

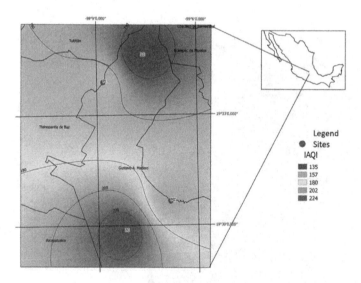

Fig. 9. Heat-maps of IAQI from the four study sites. Made with QGIS using Kriging technique.

however, this site presents some irregular urban settlements, besides on the Mexico-Pachuca highway is bordering this study site, which has a high vehicular transit [23]. Therefore, it is possible to say that due to the characteristics and anthropogenic activities carried out at both study sites, these have the worst air quality and therefore the worst biological condition.

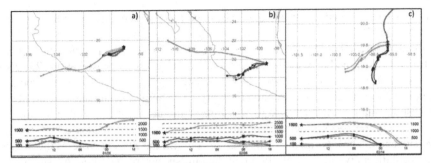

Fig. 10. HYSPLIT model runs (assuming particles as PM_{10} and $PM_{2.5}$) from the study sites, in a three-day monitoring a) January 28, 2020, b) February 6, 2020 and c) February 14, 2020.

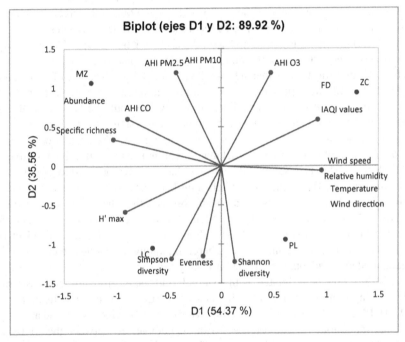

Fig. 11. Biplot of the Principal Component Analysis of the four study sites, meteorological parameters, AHI values, structural and functional diversity.

The CO, Particulate Matter, SO_2, and NO_x are known to be the main pollutants produced by mobile sources [27], which may be strongly related to the high vehicular activity of the MZ site. On the other hand, the highest mean value of temperature was found in ZC associated with the higher solar radiation that in the presence of NO_2 favors the production of O_3 [28], such a condition may explain the high values of this gas at that study site. Likewise, HYSPLIT modeling suggests that the movement of pollutants occurs from the southwest to the northeast, indicating pollutants trajectories impacting at the south of the Sierra de Guadalupe, where increased vehicular and anthropogenic activity is concentrated, contributing to raising pollutant concentrations in the southern sites (MZ and ZC).

On the other hand, the LC and PL sites are located within the polygon of the PNA Sierra de Guadalupe/La Armella, the predominant land use is conservation [23] also, anthropogenic activities are minor which, is related to the highest values of structural diversity (Simpson diversity, Shannon diversity, maximum diversity and evenness) and the best air quality (AHI and IAQI). Because of the above, it is possible to say that the sites with the best biological condition are LC and PL as they have a high species diversity and the best air quality. However, in contrast, the ZC site presents the highest functional diversity values, reflecting that the bird species recorded on this site have a lower overlap of niches and therefore use the available resources in a better mode than other study sites [8]. It is possible to state that birds can cope with adverse environmental conditions when they use the resources available in the medium appropriately.

Likewise, as mentioned above the nesting category obtained the greatest functional diversity, indicating that the bird species recorded in the four study sites have a high variety or diversity of traits associated with the species nesting type [29], such as the type of nest, the nest substrate, the number of eggs, the hatching time, among others. Therefore, it is possible to state that in general birds are taking advantage of the resources available to be able to cope with the conditions that arise and achieve reproductive success, facing various environmental conditions, which could be adverse [30]. As is the case with the ZC site, in which despite having the worst air quality and having high anthropogenic activity, functional diversity was the highest. The adaptation is defined as the anatomical, physiological and behavioral configuration of the species, given by natural selection. That is to say that the various characters are adapted to give it greater chances of survival [31]. In the case of urban birds or birds form sites that have facing alterations in natural conditions it has been observed that they carry out adaptation strategies, such as modifications in the vocalizations, which allow them to reproduce despite the high levels of noise [32, 33]. However, these studies were conducted in several surveys and at different seasons. Therefore, a long-term study in our study area is needed to identify adaptations in the bird analyzed.

The IAQI could be validated with external study sites from the ANP Sierra de Guadalupe; through bird census in different seasons. Likewise, continuous monitoring of CO, O3, PM2.5, PM10, relative humidity, wind direction, wind speed, and air temperature. Data validation will be performed with the comparison between the AHI values and an index that evaluates habitat quality, through a correlation and linear regression analysis.

6 Conclusions

The MZ and ZC study sites were the sites with the poorest air quality and biological condition, due to the geographical, climatic, and high anthropogenic activity that develops in these sites and their immediate surroundings. In contrast, the sites displaying the best air quality were the LC and PL, which have low anthropogenic activity, in addition to being immersed in the PNA polygon and support a greater structural diversity of bird communities. Also, the higher functional diversity was detected in the ZC bird community, suggesting that birds show divergence in the use of available resources in this area.

Due to the above, it is possible to claim that the PNA Sierra de Guadalupe/La Armella, which is one of the remnants of the natural sites of the CDMX, functions as a buffer zone and a remarkable biological conservation zone. Likewise, this study allows reaffirming the importance of green areas in the CDMX, since, sites such as ZC that, despite being in an urban area with industrial activity, function as a refuge for various species of birds. It is also possible to conclude that birds are good indicators of environmental quality, and in this case, of air quality.

On the other hand, it is possible to conclude that an integrated index of air quality (IAQI) associated with the structural and functional diversity of the bird community allows us to assess the biological condition of ecosystems and therefore allows us to alert promptly the possible damage to health, biodiversity, and ecosystems.

Acknowledgments. The authors would like to thank the staff of the Sierra de Guadalupe/La Armella Protected Natural Area for his assistance in developing off this project.

References

1. Raga, G.B., Baumgardner, D., Castro, T., Martínez-Arroyo, A., Navarro-González, R.: Mexico City air quality: a qualitative review of gas and aerosol measurements (1960–2000). Atm. Environ. **35**(23), 4041–4058 (2001). https://doi.org/10.1016/s1352-2310(01)00157-1

2. Rojas, L.R., Enciso, J.A.G.: Evolución y cambio industrial en las Zonas Metropolitanas del Valle de México y de Toluca, 1993–2008. Análisis Econ. **31**(77), 115–146 (2016)

3. Camacho Rodríguez, P.: Evaluación de las emisiones de contaminantes criterio y de gases de efecto invernadero, generadas por la actividad de la construcción de vialidades en la Zona Metropolitana del Valle de México (Doctoral dissertation) (2012)

4. Ballester, F.: Contaminación atmosférica, cambio climático y salud. Rev. Esp. Salud. Pública **79**, 159–175 (2005). https://doi.org/10.1590/s1135-57272005000200005

5. López-Islas, M.E., Ibarra-Meza, I., Ortiz-Ordóñez, E., Favari, L., Sedeño-Díaz, J.E., López-López, E.: Liver histopatology, lipidperoxidation and somatic indices of Fulica americana in Xochimilco (Urban) and Tecocomulco (Rural) Wetlands in the Mexico basin/histopatología del higado. Int. J. Morphol. **34**(2), 522–533 (2016). https://doi.org/10.4067/s0717-950220 16000200019

6. Sanderfoot, O.V., Holloway, T.: Air pollution impacts on avian species via inhalation exposure and associated outcomes. Environ. Res. Lett. **12**(8), 083002 (2017). https://doi.org/10.1088/1748-9326/aa8051

7. Ladin, Z.S., et al.: Using regional bird community dynamics to evaluate ecological integrity within national parks. Ecosphere **7**(9), 1–15 (2016). https://doi.org/10.1002/ecs2.1464

8. Alexandrino, E.R., et al.: Bird based Index of Biotic Integrity: Assessing the ecological condition of Atlantic Forest patches in human-modified landscape. Ecol. Ind. **73**, 662–675 (2017). https://doi.org/10.1016/j.ecolind.2016.10.023

9. Soto Coballes, N.V.: Medio siglo de monitoreo de la contaminación atmosférica en la Ciudad de México 19960-2009: aspectos científicos y sociales (Tesis de Maestría, Consejo Nacional de Ciencia y Tecnología) (2010)

10. Vázquez, R.T.: El IMECA: Indicador del Grado de Contaminación de la Atmósfera. Conciencia Tecnol. **31**, 50–53 (2006)

11. Stein, A.F., Draxler, R.R., Roph, G.D., Stunder, B.J., Cohen, M.D., Ngan, F.: NOAA's HYS-PLIT atmospheric transport and dispersion modeling system. Bull. Amer. Meteor. Soc. **96**(12), 2059–2077 (2015). https://doi.org/10.1175/bams-d-14-00110.1
12. Perevochtchikova, M.: La situación actual del sistema de monitoreo ambiental en la Zona Metropolitana de la Ciudad de México. Estud. Demográficos Urbanos, 513–547 (2009). https://doi.org/10.24201/edu.v24i3.1327
13. Stolz, T., Huertas, M.E., Mendoza, A.: Assessment of air quality monitoring networks using an ensemble clustering method in the three major metropolitan areas of Mexico. Atmos. Poll. Res. **11**, 1271–1280 (2020). https://doi.org/10.1016/j.apr.2020.05.005
14. García-Franco, J.L.: Air quality in Mexico City during the fuel shortage of January 2019. Atmos. Environ. **222**, 117–131 (2020). https://doi.org/10.1016/j.atmosenv.2019.117131
15. Borsdorff, T., Garcia Reynoso, A., Stremme, W., Grutter, M., Landgraf, J.: Monitoring CO emissions from urban districts in Mexico City using about 2 years of TROPOMI CO observations. In: EGU General Assembly Conference Abstracts, p. 5594 (2020)
16. Ochoa, E.P.: Aves silvestres como bioindicadores de contaminación ambiental y metales pesados. CES Salud Pública **5**(1), 59–69 (2014)
17. Munyenyembe, F., Harris, J., Hone, J., Nix, H.: Determinants of bird populations in an urban area. Aust. J. Ecol. **14**(4), 549–557 (1989). https://doi.org/10.1111/j.1442-9993.1989.tb01460.x
18. Wheeler, B.W., et al.: Beyond greenspace: an ecological study of population general health and indicators of natural environment type and quality. Int. J. Health Geogr. **14**(1), 17 (2015). https://doi.org/10.1186/s12942-015-0009-5
19. Canterbury, G.E., Martin, T.E., Petit, D.R., Petit, L.J., Bradford, D.F.: Bird communities and habitat as ecological indicators of forest condition in regional monitoring. Conserv. Biol. **14**(2), 544–558 (2000). https://doi.org/10.1046/j.1523-1739.2000.98235.x
20. Alcolado, P.M.: Conceptos e índices relacionados con la diversidad. Inst. Oceanologia **8**(9), 7–21 (1998)
21. Montes, A.S., Hubp, J.L.: Geomorfología de la Sierra de Guadalupe (al norte de la Ciudad de México) y su relación con peligros naturales. Rev. Mex. Cienc. Geol. **13**(2), 240–251 (1996)
22. Villavicencio, Á.A.: Evaluación de funciones y servicios ambientales. Parque Estatal Sierra de Guadalupe-Proyecto de conservación ecológica de la zona metropolitana del Valle de México (Doctoral dissertation, Universidad de Granada) (2007)
23. Programa de manejo del área natural protegida con categoría de zona sujeta a conservación ecológica "Sierra de Guadalupe". Secretaría de Medio Ambiente, Gaceta oficial de la Ciudad de México (2016)
24. Cruz Martínez, C.O.: Una aproximación al valor social y ambiental de las áreas verdes urbanas de la Ciudad de México (Tesina de Maestría, Centro de Investigación y Docencia Económica) (2016)
25. Devin, S., Burgeot, T., Giambérini, L., Minguez, L., Pain-Devin, S.: The integrated biomarker response revisited: optimization to avoid misuse. Environ. Sci. Pollut. Res. **21**(4), 2448–2454 (2014). https://doi.org/10.1007/s11356-013-2169-9
26. Beliaeff, B., Burgeot, T.: Integrated biomarker response: a useful tool for ecological risk assessment. Environ. Toxicol. Chem. **21**(6), 1316–1322 (2002). https://doi.org/10.1002/etc.5620210629
27. Castro Peña, P.C., Escobar Winston, L.M.: Estimación de las emisiones contaminantes por fuentes móviles a nivel nacional y formulación de lineamientos técnicos para el ajuste de las normas de emisión (Tesis de Ingeniería, Universidad La Salle Bogotá) (2006)
28. Jiménez, M.O.: Análisis de la eficacia, eficiencia y equidad de los programas para reducir las emisiones de ozono troposférico en la Ciudad de México. J. Econ. Lit. **16**(48), 239–265 (2019)

29. Vaccaro, A., Filloy, J., Bellocq, M.: What land use better preserves taxonomic and functional diversity of birds in a grassland biome? Avian Conserv. Ecol. **14**(1), 1 (2019). https://doi.org/10.5751/ace-01293-140101

30. Leaver, J., Mulvaney, J., Smith, D.A.E., Smith, Y.C.E., Cherry, M.I.: Response of bird functional diversity to forest product harvesting in the eastern cape, South Africa. For. Ecol. Manage. **445**, 82–95 (2019). https://doi.org/10.1016/j.foreco.2019.04.054

31. Gould, S.J., Lewontin, R.: La adaptación biológica. Paleobiology **8**(4), 214–223 (1982)

32. Pacheco Vargas, G.F.: Adaptación acústica en el canto de las especies de aves neotropicales Cyclarhis gujanensis e Hylophilus flavipes y sus densidades poblacionales en la zona de vida bosque seco tropical en el departamento del Tolima (Tesis de licenciatura, Universidad de Tolima) (2014)

33. León, E., Beltzer, A., Quiroga, M.: El jilguero dorado (Sicalis flaveola) modifica la estructura de sus vocalizaciones para adaptarse a hábitats urbanos. Rev. Mex. Biodivers. **85**(2), 546–552 (2014). https://doi.org/10.7550/rmb.32123

Swift UI and Their Integration to MapKit Technology as a Framework for Representing Spatial Information in Mobile Applications

Eduardo Eloy Loza Pacheco[1]([✉]) [iD], Mayra Lorena Díaz Sosa[1] [iD],
Christian Carlos Delgado Elizondo[1], and Miguel Jesús Torres Ruiz[2] [iD]

[1] Universidad Nacional Autónoma de México, Acatlán Edomex,
08544 Naucalpan de Juárez, Mexico
{eduardo.loza,mlds}@acatlan.unam.mx,
805849@pcpuma.acatlan.unam.mx
[2] Instituto Politecnico Nacional, Ciudad de México, CDMX, Mexico
mtorres@ipn.mx

Abstract. Mobile applications are becoming as complex as the kind of problems we need to solve. A normal GIS application needs to incorporate elements such as artificial intelligence more specifically, pattern recognition or machine learning, relational or non-relational databases, spatial representation, and reasoning. In addition to that, it is necessary to design and develop a mobile application to integrate all these elements. After analysis, planning, and design a company will require to develop a full team of engineers to accomplish an application. On the other hand, universities and other organizations, have additional interests. It is necessary to develop a mobile application to test a hypothesis before a large development project. The necessity is to use a technology that permits the integration of advanced technologies and programming tools in a manageable sense. Companies such as Google and Apple are reducing the gap of learning knowledge. They are developing new technologies. For example, Apple presented in 2019 at WWDC2019 and WWDC2020 a novelty technology called SwiftUI, which aims to reduce the complexity of developing a mobile application and allowing us to integrate technology such as Mapkit to represent spatial information. This work presents the advantages of using SwiftUI to integrate Mapkit as a spatial representation framework to ease the development of GIS mobile development. And focus on the problem solution, such as spatial representation and reasoning, robot planning, content image retrieval, etc.

Keywords: Swift UI · MapKit · GIS · Spatial representation

1 Introduction

Computer Science has a large variety of applications in different fields of science. For example, artificial intelligence and machine learning are topics and technologies widely used in several areas of knowledge [1]. The aim is to develop programs that can perform

© Springer Nature Switzerland AG 2020
M. F. Mata-Rivera et al. (Eds.): GIS LATAM 2020, CCIS 1276, pp. 80–91, 2020.
https://doi.org/10.1007/978-3-030-59872-3_6

representation and calculations of the information according to the necessity of the study. And to develop new way of representation [2] for the large problems we have today, for example data science. For example, in social sciences, we can create a model that study people activities [3]. In meteorology, we can represent the predictions of the weather [4]. In order to achieve computer science collaborations with all sciences is necessary to use a scientific computing approach. The definition of scientific computing is the intersection of Numerical Analysis, Modeling, and Computer Science, as we can see in Fig. 1 [5]. After we have selected a mathematical model and analyze the computational complexity to reduce error and increase performance. We can design an Algorithm so we can implement it on a computer.

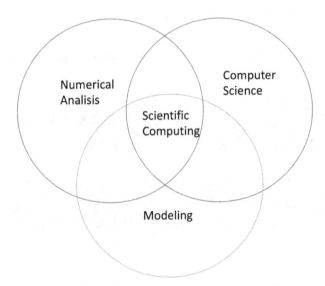

Fig. 1. Definition of scientific computing from [2].

After that, according to [6] the understanding of a computational system has three levels or layers: The concepts of computational theory we need to consider. The representation of the information or knowledge, and the design and implementation of the algorithm. And finally, the Hardware implementation. We can also add software implementation in a computer language and the use of a technological platform. In the last one, we need to consider the technical elements to improve the spatial and temporal performance of the algorithm, reduce the error, scheduling the transactions of blocks of data, access to a shared or distributed memory, etc. [7, 8]. So, we can see these as an architecture that we can use as a framework. As we can see in Fig. 2.

One of the purposes of a layered architecture is the possibility of divide activities, so we can reduce the complexity of the modules, specialize, and reuse. The communication between layers should be simple and easy. As an example, we have the architecture of the Open System Interconnection, where every layer is defined to provide one service. For example, the 5-layer hybrid model. Layers provide the service of packing, routing over the network, synchronization and codifying frames [7]. Finally, the communication

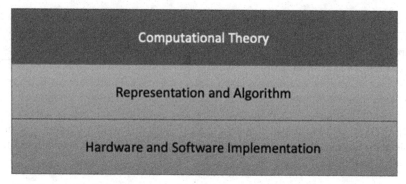

Fig. 2. Architecture of a computational system implementation according to [3].

between layers is made by an interface. In Fig. 3 we can see a general model a layered architecture.

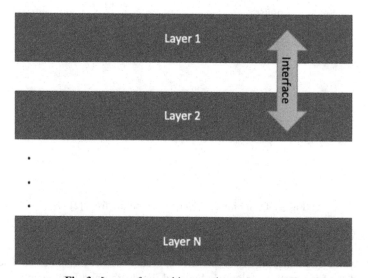

Fig. 3. Layer of an architecture image base on [7].

1.1 Brief State of the Art of User Interfaces

As mentioned before, every layer performs a function. These functions must be transparent for the other layers. So, the interfaces are the key to their communication. In the case of development platforms such as Android, Eclipse, and XCode. All of them have a Graphic User Interface (GUI) that eases the programming [9] and allows to focus in the programmer [10] and increase the productivity [11]. By making the process of development more intuitive. In the case of Xcode is integrating a new Technology called SwiftUI. Arrived in 2019 which is a declarative form of development applications [12,

13]. The declarative model is now used in major technologies such as Xamarin, UWP, and WPF with XAML [14] with the intention to simplify tasks [15]. This 2020 Apple announced new novelties at WWDC 2020 [16], with new features for the stack mode. These interfaces provide a way to progressively add functionalities. Allow us to develop algorithms as a Lego blocks. One of the interesting features are the possibility to avoid and reduce the need to manage technical details. The advantage is that we can develop advance mobile applications with high-end technology.

2   Methodology

The proposed methodology is agile. The intention is to focus on the development of the three parts which are design, implementation, and feedback. The advantages of this approach are. that we can integrate modules gradually to the architecture such as reconfigure the presentation or add another functionality to the applications. As it seems in Sect. 4.1. The methodology for example also allows reconfiguring the applications in a short period of time, whether it is needed to add elements to the GIS functionality or change the technology from Mapkit to ArcGis without affecting other elements in the project (Fig. 4).

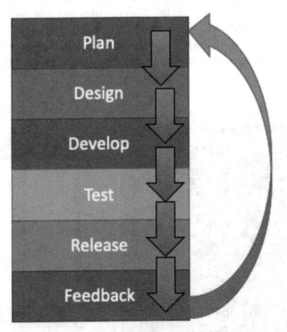

Fig. 4. AGILE development methodology

3   Standard Mobile Implementation of MapKit on XCode

XCode allows the development by using a mechanism called a storyboard. This is made by a file called Main.storyboard. Which represents the structure of the objects and their distribution in the mobile device. As it seems in Xcode the working area of Xcode on the left have file hierarchy section where we can select any file of the project. There's also an edit section where the code can be modified. The file ViewController.swift controls the behavior of the application. Finally, Xcode shows a graphic representation of the Main.storyboard. Where we can insert objects such as buttons, images, and maps and place them where they are suitable. The project needs to be compiled to run in the simulator or an external device. This program is called Simulator. Xcode allows selecting the specific device where the application is designed to be executed. For example, iPad, iPad Pro, iPhone X, iPhone 8, etc. It is important to mention that every time we need to see the result of output. It has to be executed the simulator or the external device. The problem with compiling every time is that if we need to see a minor change, is to spend more time in compiling. As a result, it loses the sense of being programming in real-time.

4   Implementation Using SwiftUI on Xcode

On the other hand, we have a new technology of GUI called SwiftUI. Similar to Main.storyboard. But with new characteristics that permits the development be more dynamically. In Fig. 5 on the left are the working files and edit code (left and center respectively). On the right there is a novelty. A simulation of a mobile phone where every time a change is done in the left a change is reflected on the simulated phone. As was previously described in the last section this model allows also to run the Simulator program.

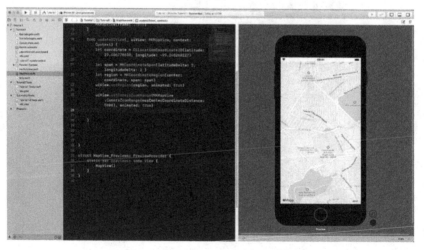

Fig. 5. SwiftUI graphic interface on Xcode.

One of the features of this technology is that it is possible to build all the components the application needs independently. Which eases the modularity. In addition to that, it allows to create systems and algorithms more robust [8]. Increase cohesion and reduce the coupling of the modules. These are valuable to detect errors easily [17]. That is because the constructions of the elements in SwiftUI use verticals and horizontals stacks structures (Vstack and HStack). In the WWDC2020 introduce an enhance of these structures. As it is shown in Fig. 6 the structures can be nested. In addition to that SwiftUI manages almost automatically the alignment of the elements. So, there is less need to program restrictions. In Fig. 7 we can see the automatic align in a vertical and horizontal position.

```
ScrollView {
    VStack {
        MapView().frame(height:300)
        SwiftUIView().offset(y:-130).padding(
            .bottom,-130)
        VStack {
            Text("UNAM-FES").font(.title)
                .foregroundColor(.blue)


        }
        HStack {
            Text("Matemáticas").font(.subheadline)
            Spacer()
            Text("Computación")


        }
        .padding()
    }
}
```

Fig. 6. Use of Stacks and ScrollView.

4.1 Geographical Implementation Using MapKit and SwiftUI

Suppose our application must add a geographical representation. So, we need to use MapKit. We can divide the application in four parts. One part can describe the distribution of the elements in the phone, similar to HTML. Then we add a functionality or some other elements to the application. We have a module that manages the geographical representation and receive geographical data, longitude and latitude. Finally, a layer that processes the data. In the Fig. 8, we can see the architecture that can be used interchangeably to add the functionality we need. We can see that at the top of the stack we find the Application representation.

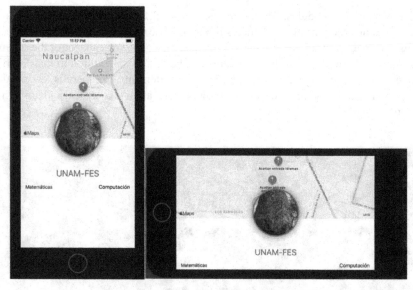

Fig. 7. A vertical and horizontal simulation of an mobile phone.

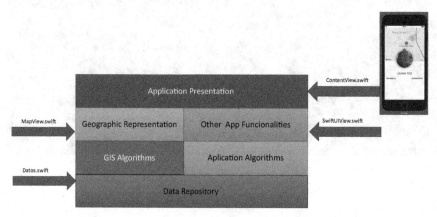

Fig. 8. An architecture for a general geographic application.

4.2 Data Structures Such as GEO JASON or SHAPEFILES

For the manipulation of the Map we have a file that contains all code related to the Maps management. In this case, it is called MapView. And it is important to import the libraries SwiftUI and MapKit and extend the class UIViewRepresentable. The file allows us to represent the geographic locations as it seems in Fig. 9. In SwiftUI, we can add new locations and we will see the change on the right. (The location Added is UNAM-FES Acatlán.).

Then we can add another swift file (In this case SwiftUIView.swift), to add a functionality. In this case we only are interested in adding an image. The result is observed

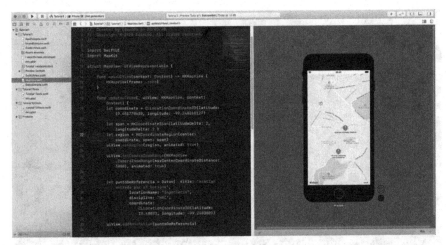

Fig. 9. Adding a map and showing the results on the right.

on the right in the Fig. 9. For this example, the processing of the data is static. But for other applications it is possible to use a database, a GEOJson file (Fig. 10), storing data on the device, etc. The structure uses a class model called DataModel.swift to store the receiving information. The file needs to import the MapKit library so we can use the objects of CLLocationCoordinate and MKAnnotation [18–20]. We also have the option to manipulate shape files. Because as it seems in their technical description [21]. It can be processed as a structure to use it as a Polygon or Multipoint. Now there are also work in ArCGIS to connect it to iOS such as [22] and use it in the ArcGIS implementation in our proposed architecture.

The final result is showed in Fig. 11. Where the ContentView integrates all the elements.

4.3   Similarities Between Main.Storyboard and SwiftUI

However, it is not necessary to learn new concepts. Whether you are familiarized with Swift and XCode environment. For SwiftUI the structure MKMapView use the function updateUIView(). The function processes the map. And it is possible to set and get elements from MKMapView (such as longitude, latitude, region, zoom). See Fig. 12a).

```
8   import MapKit
9
10  class DataModel: NSObject, MKAnnotation {
11      let title: String?
12      let locationName: String?
13      let discipline: String?
14      let coordinate: CLLocationCoordinate2D
15
16
17      init(
18          title: String?,
19          locationName: String?,
20          discipline: String?,
21          coordinate: CLLocationCoordinate2D){
22
23          self.title = title
24          self.locationName = locationName
25          self.discipline = discipline
26          self.coordinate = coordinate
27
28          super.init()
29
30      }
```

Fig. 10. Class DataModel.

In the case of the Main.storyboard the same methods and properties are used (region, location, span). In this case, there were written in the function viewDidLoad(). To load the map after the application is executed. The difference is that we have to add manually an *outlet* to communicate the Main.storyboard to the ViewController.swift. As it seems on line 15 in the following Fig. 12b).

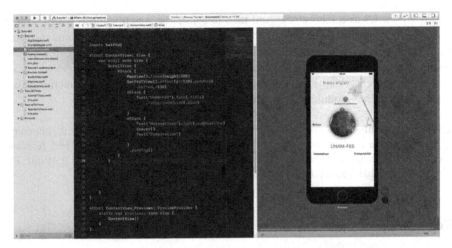

Fig. 11. The integration of all elements on the ContentView.swift.

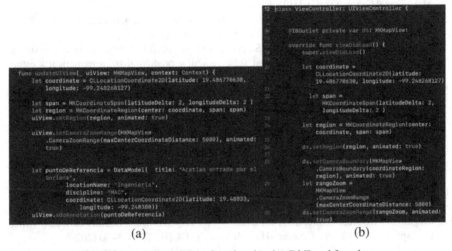

Fig. 12. a) updateUIView function, b) viewDidLoad function

5   Conclusions

We can see that a simple implementation can be developed with SwiftUI. SwiftUI offers us a high level of characteristics like WYSIWYG. Because as we are implementing a section of code, we can see the result in real-time. This is very helpful when we are searching for accelerated results or testing a functionality. On the other hand, is clear that an application more extensive will require more degree of expressiveness that Main.storyboard can offer. But these two forms of development are not exclusive of any implementation. All the code made in SwiftUI is functional and easily adapted to traditional modality (Main.storyboard) and vice versa. Once you have an algorithm in one version, it can be translated into another. The intention of using this framework is to use SwiftUI as a laboratory. And then integrate the functionalities with a major application or system, isolating possible errors. In addition to that as it was mention in the introduction, now major technologies are used declarative language to ease the development. Summarizing we can see that SwiftUI offers a functional user experience. The Architecture divided into layers is useful to trace errors and add functionalities without affect other modules.

Acknowledgements. The authors would like to thank to the Universidad Nacional Autónoma de México and the Department of Applied Mathematics and Computer Science of FES Acatlán, The "Consejo Nacional de Ciencia y Tecnología" of México. and DGAPA-UNAM (PAPIME PE 304717) for the funds to support this work.

References

1. Theobald, O.: Machine Learning for Absolute Beginners (2017)
2. Bernstein, G.L., Kjolstad, F.: Perspectives: why new programming languages for simulation? ACM Trans. Graph. (TOG) **35**(2), 1–3 (2016)
3. Sarker, I.: Exploiting data-centric social context in phone call prediction: a machine learning based study. EAI Endorsed Trans. Scalable Inf. Syst. **6**(20) (2019)
4. Aybar-Ruiz, A., Jiménez-Fernández, S., et al.: A novel grouping genetic algorithm–extreme learning machine approach for global solar radiation prediction from numerical weather models inputs. Solar Energy **132**, 129–142 (2016)
5. Karniadakis, G., Robert, M., Kirby II, M.: Parallel Scientific Computing in C ++ and MPI. Cambridge University Press (2003)
6. Alpaydin, E.: Machine Learning, pp. 48–49. MIT Press (2016)
7. Tanenbaum, A., Wetheall, D.: Computer Networks. Pearson (2013)
8. Levitin, A.: Introduction to the Design & Analysis of Algorithms, Boston (2012)
9. Inie, N., Dalsgaard, P.: How interaction designers use tools to manage ideas. ACM Trans. Comput.-Hum. Interact. (TOCHI) **27**(2), 1–26 (2020)
10. Dix, A.: Human–computer interaction, foundations and new paradigms. J. Vis. Lang. Comput. **42**, 122–134 (2017)
11. Mcgill, M., Kehoe, A., Freeman, E., Brewster, S.: Expanding the bounds of seated virtual workspaces. ACM Trans. Comput.-Hum. Interact. (TOCHI) **27**(3), 1–40 (2020)
12. Apple. Inc.: Xcode - SwiftUI- Apple Developer. https://developer.apple.com/xcode/swiftui/. Accessed 28 June 2020
13. Apple. Inc.: Introducing Swift UI, v. https://developer.apple.com/tutorials/swiftui. Accessed 28 June 2020
14. Microsoft 2020. *Xamarin.Forms | .NET*. https://dotnet.microsoft.com/apps/xamarin/xamarin-forms. Accessed 28 June 2020
15. Heer, J., Bostock, M.: Declarative language design for interactive visualization. IEEE Trans. Visual Comput. Graphics **16**(6), 1149–1156 (2010)
16. Apple WWDC 2020. https://developer.apple.com/videos/play/wwdc2020/10031. Accessed 27 June 2020
17. Singh, Y., Malhotra, R.: Object Oriented Software Engineering. PHH, India (2012)
18. Raywenderlich. https://www.raywenderlich.com/3715234-swiftui-getting-started. Accessed 27 June 2020
19. Hacking with swift. https://www.hackingwithswift.com/books/ios-swiftui/integrating-map kit-with-swiftui. Accessed 27 June 2020

20. Apple Inc. https://developer.apple.com/documentation/mapkit/mkannotation. Accessed 27 June 2020
21. ESRI. ESRI Shapefile Technical Description (1998)
22. ArcGIS Runtime SDK Samples. App Store (2020). https://apps.apple.com/us/app/arcgis-run time-sdk-samples/id1180714771?mt=8. Accessed 24 July 2020

Forecasting People's Influx on Mexico City Metrobus Line 1 Using a Fractal Analysis

Vladimir Avalos-Bravo[1]([⊠]) [ID], Chadwick Carreto Arellano[2] [ID],
Diego Alfredo Padilla Pérez[3] [ID], and Macario Hernández Cruz[4] [ID]

[1] Instituto Politécnico Nacional, DEV, SEPI-ESIQIE, SARACS Research Group ESIME
Zacatenco, Mexico City, Mexico
ravalos@ipn.mx
[2] Instituto Politécnico Nacional, DEV, SEPI-ESCOM, Mexico City, Mexico
chadcarreto@gmail.com
[3] Instituto Politécnico Nacional, CDA, SARACS Research Group ESIME Zacatenco,
Mexico City, Mexico
padilla.diego@outlook.com
[4] Instituto Politécnico Nacional, DEV, Mexico City, Mexico
mahernandezc@ipn.mx

Abstract. Metrobus Line 1 user's influx has increased significantly year by year since its operations beginning at 2005, the amount of Metrobus users increase day by day in every line, even with new routes and most BRT unit, it menas that Metrobus system has not a prospective model to determine the amount of users that the system will have every month and with this information, stablish an improvement planning to avoid user's delays. This paper presents a fractal analysis of Metrobus line 1 users influx as a forecast model that allows us to know the people increase and the impact it will have in the future to help in the decision making process with an ARFIMA model to predict Metrobus Line 1 user's monthly influx for every month during years 2020, 2021 and 2022, analyzing their behavior Metrobus line 1 infrastructure planning including rides, stations extension and user's limit can be improved.

Keywords: Forecast · Fractals · ARFIMA · BRT · Mexico City

1 Introduction

According to Metrobus webpage, the central part of a city development is an effective public transport system. For most of cities population, public transportation is the only way to access employment, education and public services [1]. This means that a set of movements of people are made through various modes of transport [2]. Thus, at the end of the day, literally millions of journeys in our city are produced.

Another definition is the movement of people from one point to another and regardless of the means by which it moves, has different consequences to them, because of this, it is desirable to separate the consequences into two groups: the consumption of resources

M. F. Mata-Rivera et al. (Eds.): GIS LATAM 2020, CCIS 1276, pp. 92–105, 2020.
https://doi.org/10.1007/978-3-030-59872-3_7

and environmental impacts [2]. The word mobility means in extension the consumption of various non-material and material resources. The first consumption is non-material and is related to the time people spent moving from one point to another, the time is a non-renewable and worthy resource for people. Reducing travel time to the lowest possible level will always be the goal of transport service users. Second one is space, mobility requires space in order to build the transport infrastructure and space when people use it. I.e. sidewalks, freeways, bus terminals, railway stations and railways that occupy a huge physical space, cost of construction and maintenance is paid by society through their taxes. In the other hand, people consume different amounts of road space when they are using different modes of transportation and consume energy, which is wasted by all motorized or electrified vehicles, it is worth mentioning that public transport such as metro and trolleybus uses electricity, while the BRT systems, in Mexico City case called Metrobus and private vehicles, use fuel. And the third one is the financial resource, i.e. road maintenance costs, traffic signals and operation, the living of the police assigned to these tasks and, in the case of owners of means of transport, maintenance of the same.

1.1 Mobility Transport Problems and Bus Rapid Transit System (BRT)

The movement of people from one point to another and regardless of the transport means by which it moves, has different consequences for those who live in the same environment that is why it is convenient to separate these consequences into two groups: resource consumption and environmental impacts.

Talking about mobility is necessary to talk about the consumption of various tangible and intangible assets. The first intake is not material and is related to the time spent in traveling from one point to another, since time is a nonrenewable resource for people. Reducing travel time to a minimum is always the objective of the transport services users. The second one is the space, mobility demands space when it is necessary to build the transport infrastructure and when people use that infrastructure. Examples are, sidewalks, highways, bus terminals, train stations and railways that occupy a large physical space, the cost of construction and maintenance is paid by the society through their taxes. In the second case, people consume different amounts of circulating space when they are using different ways of transportation. The third one is the energy consumed by all motorized or electrified vehicles including public transportation such as subways and trolleybus that uses electricity, meanwhile Metrobus and private vehicles, as well as private transport use fuel. The fourth one is financial resources, such as road maintenance costs, signs and traffic operation, talking about the police entrusted with the transport tasks and in the case of the transport means owners, the maintenance [2].

The use of motorized vehicles involves several forms of atmospheric and sound pollution too, six types of air pollution related to transportation are identified [3]:

a) Sensitive contamination: perceived by people through the smell and vision because the source is close to the person.
b) Contamination affecting human health: The presence of pollutants such as CO, nitrogen oxides and hydrocarbons.
c) Photochemical Smog: The presence of contaminants in the atmosphere.
d) Acid rain: The main consequence is the damage caused to forest areas.

e)   Effect of the ozone layer on the planet's poles.
f)   Greenhouse effect, caused mainly by CO_2 concentration in the atmosphere.

1.2   Traffic Congestion

Traffic congestion is a condition that occurs in the roads and characterized by very low speeds, detriment in travel times, and considerable increase of vehicles lines [4, 5]. There are a number of specific circumstances that generate or aggravate congestion; for example, the volume of traffic, works on roads, weather events (e.g., flooding roadways) and most of them attributed to the occurrence of road accidents. The traffic road research has revealed that still cannot fully predict in what conditions suddenly a traffic jam can occur [5]. However, it has been found that accidents can cause cascading failures that spread to other roads later (and other modes) and create a sustained traffic jam [4, 5]. It is clear that traffic congestion has a number of negative effects [6]:

a)   waste of time for drivers and passengers; i.e. as a productive activity for most people, congestion reduces economic health of the city;
b)   delays, which can lead to late arrival of employees to meetings and education, resulting in lost for business, disciplinary measures and other personal losses.
c)   fuel waste and increased CO_2 emissions, causing air pollution due to increased 'renteli', acceleration and braking;
d)   issues on emergencies: blocked traffic can interfere with the emergency vehicles circulation when they are traveling to their destinations where are urgently needed;
e)   high probability of collisions due to the space between vehicles and trucks as well as the constant stops and 'starts' to advance during a road congestion.

2   Urban Mobility in Mexico City BRT System

Urban mobility, is still dominated by the "car culture" [7]. Motorized models, on the other hand, produce air and noise pollution as well as accidents and congestion. In the late 90's and early XXI century, Mexico City had been affected by the lack of efficient transport services.

This is due to excessive population growth in the city and traffic problems in main avenues for the huge number of cars and the collapse in the urban transport system [8]. In the year 2005 starts the new massive transport system called Metrobus along one of the main avenues with 30 km long (Metrobus line 1). It is believed that Metrobus system improved mobility by 50%; given immediate benefits of mobility, thousands of users decided to make a modal shift from private vehicles to public transport. The success of line 1 led to the opening of more lines, as the lines 2 (2008), 3 (2011), 4 (2012), 5 (2013), 6 (2016) 7 (2018). Other extensions area planned and under construction. Currently, the seven lines together cover a length 140 km over Mexico City and carrying about 1, 400,000 users daily (See Table 1) [9].

Traffic accidents are a serious public health problem. They are the leading cause of death among 15–44 aged men and the fifth leading cause of death for women in the

Table 1. Some features of Mexico City Metrobus Transport System

Features	L1	L2	L3	L4	L5	L6	L7	Total
Length	30 km	20 km	17 km	28 km	10 km	20 km	15 km	140 km
Operations start	June 2005	Dec 2009	Feb 2011	April 2012	Nov 2013	Jan 2016	Feb 2018	–
Stations	44	34	29	32	16	35	29	219
Users/Day	480000	180000	140000	65000	55000	150000	130000	1,4000,000

same range. A 2004 World Health Organization report states that 1.2 million of deaths worldwide occur because of traffic accidents, with more than 50 million people injured.

The costs of accidents are extremely high and are 1% to 2% of countries' Gross Domestic Product. The estimated annual cost around the world is USD 518 billion and is concentrated in the rich countries of high motorization. Despite this, all studies show that the problem tends to worsen in developing countries, as the motorization of their societies grows, especially when the transit environment and the society itself are not prepared for this sudden increase [10].

In order to carry out an exhaustive review concerning the constant accidents that occur in BRT systems and the way in which these affect the urban mobility and the potential users, it is important to consider that a greater part of the Mexico City BRT system accidents occurs at intersections, either due to vehicular and pedestrian influx or other factors [11].

Consulted data sources are reports obtained through infomex web page [12–17], provided by the public security secretary, Metrobus system reports, newspapers articles, collision videos of video streaming sites and other electronic media from 2005 to present [18–20]. Research on BRT has been reported in literature of several issues; for example, from an economic perspective [6, 21, 23, 35], social perspective [22, 27–29, 31], technical performance [23–26, 30], environmental perspective [21, 34], road safety [24, 36] and accident analysis [18–20], however, there are few studies being conducted explicitly on BRT user's mobility forecast [36–40], data analysis or improvement [32, 33].

According to this, it is necessary to predict the number of users in order to avoid congestions in the BRT stations due users at different peak hours, (see Table 2).

Metrobus line 1 have three peak hours per day every week:

'Peak-Hours' (PH) in Line 1:
06:00 hrs ≤ PH-Early Morning ≤ 08:00 hrs
13:00 hrs ≤ PH-Afternoon ≤ 15:00 hrs
17:00 hrs ≤ PH-Until Early/Night ≤ 20:00 hrs

Artificial Neural Networks (ANN) are a good mathematical tool for forecasting, but one of ANN limitations is that a big amount of historical data is required to train it; therefore, it gives guideline of not selecting ANN to make forecast of Metrobus Line 1 user's influx instead of fractals, that have an advantage on analyzing smaller amounts of historical data and they are an excellent tool for this cases.

Table 2. Mexico City Metrobus Transport System line 1 users per year [8, 9].

2005	37,049,149
2006	74,321,914
2007	77,505,395
2008	89,201,679
2009	93,455,128
2010	99,342,235
2011	109,164,875
2012	122,082,471
2013	124,891,960
2014	127,044,608
2015	133,475,705
2016	135,570,009
2017	136,980,154
2018	152,395,710
2019	157,256,938
Total users	**1,669,737,930**

3 Methodology

To focus on influx for years 2020, 2021 and 2022 of Metrobus Transport System, the Fractal Dimension "D" will be used. The Fractal Dimension is a numerical quantity that serves to characterize and even classify fractal objects, a generalization of the Euclidean dimension, so an object is fractal only when its dimension is greater than its Euclidean dimension and allow us to determine if model can be used with history of total monthly user influx from 2008 to 2019 data. Besides, fractal dimension is the main element to apply ARFIMA model to historical data and know Metrobus Line 1 influx forecast, the fractal dimension (D) is given by:

$$D = 2 - H \ || \ H = Hurst \ Coefficient \tag{1}$$

It means:

$$d = H - \frac{1}{2} \tag{2}$$

Where
d = Fractional integration parameter
H = Hurst coefficient

The fractional integration parameter (d) establishes the following behaviors for the time series:

- If $0 < d < 0.5$ the Auto Regression, Fractional Integration and Moving Average (ARFIMA) process is a stationary process of long-term memory. In this case, the auto-correlations are positive and decrease hyperbolically towards 0 depending on the delay.
- If $d = 0$ the ARFIMA process is reduced to an ARMA process, and does not present any long-term memory structure.
- If $-0.5 < d < 0$ the ARFIMA process is an antipersistent process. In this case, the autocorrelations alternate the sign.

To calculate Fractal dimension (D) Benoit 1.2 software is used, it is a commercial computer program that enables to measure the fractal dimension and/or hurst exponent of data sets using different methods in for 2D data such as ruler, box, information, perimeter-area, and mass for analysis of self-similar patterns; Fractal Dimension D is obtained with Box-Dimension technique based on the history of total monthly user influx from 2008 to 2019. Once fractional integration parameter (D) is available, the ARFIMA model will be applied in ITSM2000 commercial software.

3.1 Influx User's Analysis

The calculation of the fractal dimension (D) uses the Box-Dimension technique of the influx of Metrobus. Line 1 with the historical data of Table 2, The historical data was plotted in Excel because the software only can read data in bmp format, so it was saved as a bmp fil using paint software (See Fig. 1).

$$Hurst\ Coefficient\ (H) = 2 - D = 2 - (1.43009) \tag{3}$$

Thus:

$$Fractal\ Dimension\ (D) = 1.43009 \tag{4}$$

To calculate Fractional Integration Parameter:

$$(d) = H - \frac{1}{2} = 0.56991 - \frac{1}{2} = 0.06991 \tag{5}$$

Thus, Fractional Integration Parameter (d) is in the following range:

$$0 > d < \frac{1}{2} \tag{6}$$

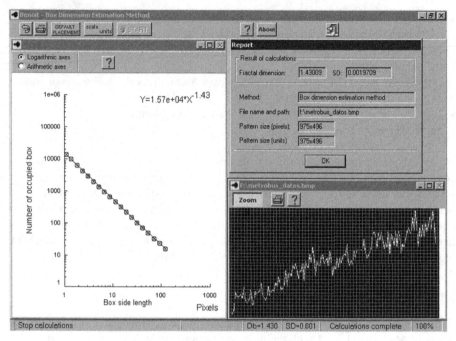

Fig. 1. Calculation of fractal dimension.

ARFIMA is a steady process with long term memory

Based on the integration parameter, ARFIMA model is generated. For ARFIMA model, a transformation is required to remove the growth or decrease, trend and periodicity of the time series with a Box-Cox of level 0.1.

```
==========================================
```
ITSM::(Maximum likelihood estimates)
```
==========================================
```
Method: Maximum Likelihood
ARMA Model:

ARMA Model:
$(1-B)^{.06991}[X(t) - .8681 X(t-1) - .02606 X(t-2) - .1823 X(t-3) + .6081 X(t-4)$
$- .4987 X(t-5) + .2424 X(t-6) - .1104 X(t-7) + .1074 X(t-8)$
$- .1527 X(t-9) + .2353 X(t-10) - .3796 X(t-11) - .3743 X(t-12)$
$+ .5283 X(t-13)]$
$= Z(t) - .5389 Z(t-1) - .008898 Z(t-2) - .4969 Z(t-3)$
$+ .7616 Z(t-4)$
WN Variance = .000000

AR Coefficients

.868140	.026059	.182339	-.608053
.498747	-.242412	.110447	-.107392
.152661	-.235265	.379611	.374306
-.528275			

MA Coefficients

-.538930	-.008898	-.496934	.761641

(Residual SS)/N = .0827473

AIC = .111000E+33

-2Log(Likelihood) (Whittle) = .111000E+33

Sequentially, the residuals of data series are analyzed, analyzing to what degree the model obtained is valid for the monthly influx of Metrobus users. the graph of the simple autocorrelation function (ACF) and the partial autocorrelation function (PACF) based on the inflow data is shown below (See Fig. 2).

It is observed that more than 95% of the data are within the confidence bands, therefore, the data come from an independent and identically distributed series (i.i.d). The residuals of data series should also be analyzed using the residual analysis and randomness test. The analysis is shown below.

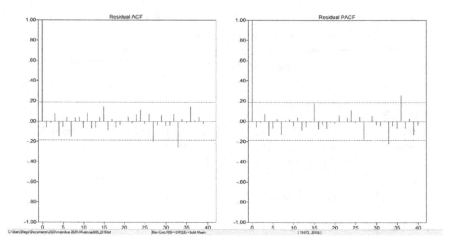

Fig. 2. ACF/PACF residuals.

```
=================================================
ITSM::(Tests of randomness on residuals)
=================================================
```

Ljung - Box statistic = 43.078 Chi-Square (20), p-value = 0.00200
McLeod - Li statistic = 23.623 Chi-Square (37), p-value = 0.95688
Turning points = 74.000~AN(72.667,sd = 4.4058), p-value = 0.76217
Diff sign points = 49.000~AN(55.000,sd = 3.0551), p-value = 0.04953
Rank test statistic = .29350E+04~AN(.30525E+04,sd = .19620E+03), p-value = .54926
Jarque-Bera test statistic (for normality) = .054737 Chi-Square (2), p-value = 0.97300

```
Order of Min AICC YW Model for Residuals = 0
```

Tests of randomness on residuals contrasts that the model passes one of the randomness tests, but by virtue of passing at least one McLeod-Li, the model can be taken as valid; this indicates that the probability of observing these data assuming that the hypothesis of the data comes from a series i.i.d. is 0.95688. It is imperative to perform the Goodness of Fit to know the behavior of the ARFIMA model to know the fit that it has throughout the time series. Figure 3 shows the inflow data versus the ARFIMA model.

Based on residuals between influx data and ARFIMA model, the goodness of fit is obtained

The Average Error (ME) (See Table 3), which indicates the approximation of the ARFIMA model based on the data. The Mean of the Absolute Value of Error (MAE) which provides the comparison of the ARFIMA model with respect to the real data. The Sum of the Error Square (SSE) and the Mean Square Error (MSE) indicate the dispersions. This reflects the separation of the ARFIMA model from its central point. The Standard Deviation of Error (SDE) which determines the average of the fluctuations of the ARFIMA model with respect to the real inflow data. The Estimate Error Bias (UM) this must be close to zero. If UM > 0.2, another model must be proposed. Variability

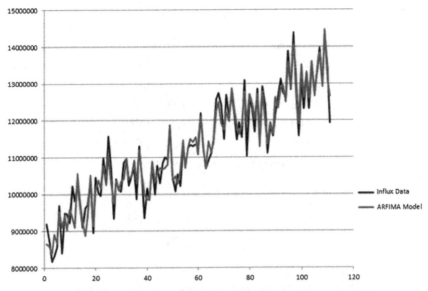

Fig. 3. Influx data versus ARFIMA model.

Model (US) shows the ability of proposed ARFIMA model to replicate variability degree against actual data flow. Variability degree is in the range from 0 to 1, with zero being the maximum variability. The non-systematic error or remaining error (UC) represents the divergence values of ARFIMA model with actual "Correlation" data. Finally, the Theil's U which is the sum of (UM) 2 + (US) 2 + (UC) 2 which compares the growths of the ARFIMA model against real influx data, using fluctuations of zero (maximum coincidence) and 1 (maximum divergence). Therefore, it has been verified based on goodness of fit, the ACF/PACF graphs and the randomness residuals test of ARFIMA model is adequate to forecast monthly influx of Metrobus Line 1 users for 2020, 2021 and 2022 years. The forecast for the monthly Influx of Metrobus Line 1 for years 2020, 2021 and 2022 in red and green in color (See Fig. 4).

4   Discussion and Results

The forecast of Mexico City Metrobus line 1 monthly influx for years 2020, 2021 and 2022 based on Fig. 4 are shown below:

It is worth mentioning that the forecast of year 2020 influx for March, April, May and June months are limited to 50%; July is calculated at 60%; August was projected at 70%; September focused on 80% of the total influx due to COVID-19 confinement and the Government restrictions.

Table 3. Goodness of fit

Goodness of fit	
ME	-1.41×10^4
MAE	2.58×10^5
SSE	1.15×10^{13}
MSE	1.04×10^{11}
SDE	3.24×10^5
Correlation Coefficient	0.9731
U	8.08×10^{-4}
U_M	1.24×10^{-3}
U_S	1.71×10^{-3}
U_C	2.84×10^{-2}

Table 4. Forecast of Mexico City Metrobus line 1 monthly influx

Forecast of Metrobus line 1 influx			
Month	Year 2020	Year 2021	Year 2022
January	11361169	13651499	13372879
February	11891641	13448016	14678055
March	13814542	14398947	14498099
April	12891010	14085587	15248697
May	12983147	14814618	15930254
June	13020088	14841871	15292412
July	13499818	15697123	16385200
August	14429980	15015049	15878766
September	13074478	13961059	14273695
October	14273703	15510534	13436573
November	13377996	14524632	13857265
December	12339324	14388168	15231780

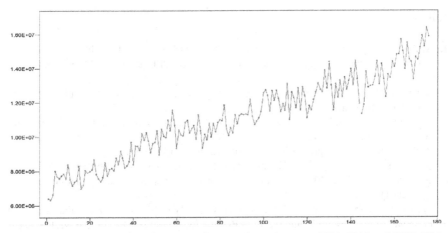

Fig. 4. Forecast of the monthly Influx of Metrobus line 1 for years 2020, 2021 and 2022. (Color figure online)

5 Conclusions

This paper has shown a forecast based on ARFIMA model in order to predict Metrobus Line 1 user's monthly influx for every month during years 2020, 2021 and 2022. Metrobus Line 1 user's influx has increased significantly year by year since its operations beginning at 2005. Influx increase give the guideline for analyzing their behavior for years 2020, 2021 and 2022 and the impact that the Increased influx will have on Metrobus line 1 infrastructure planning.

The main conclusions were the following:

a) ARFIMA model has a good performance in time series forecast, precising prediction of Metrobus line 1 user's influx, which will be necessary for infrastructure improvement plan.

b) Influx increase puts at risk healthy distance in Metrobus system, targeting as a high risk of contagion area, besides stealing and people assault, so it is necessary to control people access and program BRT unit's rides due people influx on Metrobus line 1 corridor.

c) Increase BRT units rides without a plan due users demand will affect traffic and normal life of potential users. The Mexico City Metrobus system should do an improvement plan on the unit's rides in order to attend the users demand and avoid saturation.

d) It is immediately required to review loading polygons to make a strategic planning for buses runs based on presented forecast due to Metrobus user's influx.

e) It is necessary to maintain emergency plans and make timely and accurate adjustments based on mobility collapse in Metrobus line 1 corridor.

Acknowledgments. This project was funded under the following grants: SIP-IPN: No-20201054, SIP-IPN: No-20201606 and the support of DEV-IPN Instituto Politecnico Nacional.

References

1. Avalos-Bravo, V., Santos-Reyes, J., Padilla-Perez, D.: BRT accidents in intersections or crossroads: a review of empirical research. In: 15th LACCEI International Multi-conference (2017)
2. Alcántara, E.: Análisis de la movilidad urbana, espacio, medio ambiente y equidad, pp. 74–111–116. Colombia, CAF (2010)
3. Jourmad, R., Paturel, L., Vidon, R., Guitton, J.-P., Saber, A.-I., Combet, E.: Emissions Unitaires de Polluants des Vehicules Legers, INRETS Report No. 116. Institut National de Recherche sur les Transports et leur Securite, Bron, France (1990)
4. American Association of State Highway and Transportation Officials Executive Committee 2000–2001 AASHTO (2001) – A Policy on Geometric Design of Highways and Streets, 4th. edn. (2001)
5. Litman, T.: Smarter Congestion Relief in Asian Cities: Win-Win Solutions to Urban Transport Problems, Transport and Communications Bulletin for Asia and the Pacific, No. 82, December 2013 (2013)
6. Levinson, H., et al.: Transit cooperative research program report 90, Bus Rapid Transit, Volume 1: case studies in Bus Rapid Transit, TRB, National Research Council, Washington, DC (2003)
7. Zhao, P.: Sustainable urban expansion and transportation in a growing megacity: consequences of urban sprawl for mobility on the urban fringe of Beijing. Habitat Int. **34**(2), 236–243 (2010)
8. INEGI Homepage. http://www.inegi.org.mx/est/contenidos/proyectos/graficas_temas/epobla02.htm?s=est&c=17510
9. BRTDATA Homepage. brtdata.org
10. Santos-Reyes, J., Avalos-Bravo, V., Padilla-Perez, D.: Bus rapid transit system road safety: a case study of Mexico City. Urban Transp. Syst. INTECH **7**, 125–141 (2016)
11. World Health Order Homepage: Global status report on road safety: time for action, Geneva. http://www.who.int/violence_injury_prevention/road_safety_status/2015/en/
12. INFOMEX: Reporte del accidente-Metrobús de la línea 2 (2014). www.infomexdf.org.mx
13. INFOMEX: Reporte del accidente del día viernes 15 de marzo de 2013 en la Av. Insurgentes casi esquina con Hamburgo (2014). www.infomexdf.org.mx
14. INFOMEX: Reporte del accidente del día miércoles 11 de julio de2012 a las 15:30 horas en el cruce de avenida Congreso de la Unión y Héroe de Nacozari (2014). www.infomexdf.org. mx
15. INFOMEX: Reporte del accidente del día miércoles 16 de julio de 2014 aproximadamente a las 11:49 a.m. cuando camión de carga con placas 614 DD7, propiedad de la empresa Fletes Chihuahua, S.A de C.V., se pasó el alto en Av. Congreso de la Unión esquina con Héroes de Nacozari impactando en el costado izquierdo de la unidad del Metrobús-542 de la línea 4 (2014). www.infomexdf.org.mx
16. INFOMEX: Reporte del accidente-Av Jalisco (2014). www.infomexdf.org.mx
17. INFOMEX: Reporte del accidente del accidente del día 13 de junio de 2015, en el cruce de Av. Insurgentes y Hamburgo (2016). www.infomexdf.org.mx
18. Avalos-Bravo, V., Santos-Reyes, J., Padilla-Perez, D.: A preliminary analysis of accident data of one of the BRT lines in Mexico City. In: ESREL 2016 (2017)
19. Avalos-Bravo, V., Santos-Reyes, J.: A preliminary analysis of two bus rapid transit accidents in Mexico City. Procedia Eng. **84**, 624–633 (2014)
20. Avalos-Bravo, V., Santos-Reyes, J.: A preliminary accident analysis of three bus rapid transit cases in Mexico City. Estudios Iberoamericanos en Ingeniería de Tránsito, Transporte y Logística, Instituto de Ingeniería UNAM, pp 879–892 (2020)

21. Cervero, R., Kang, C.D.: Bus Rapid Transit impacts on land values in Seoul Korea. Transp. Policy **18**, 102–116 (2011)
22. Delmelle, E.C., Casas, I.: Evaluating the spatial equity of bus rapid transit-based accessibility patterns in a developing country: the case of Cali, Colombia. Transp. Policy **20**, 36–46 (2012)
23. Hensher, D.A., Golob, T.F.: Bus Rapid Transit Systems: a comparative assessment. Transportation **35**, 501–518 (2008)
24. Hidalgo, D., Lleras, G., Hernandez, E.: Methodology of calculating passenger capacity in bus rapid transit systems: application to the Transmilenio system in Bogotá Colombia. Res. Transp. Econ. **39**, 139–142 (2012). http://dx.doi.org/j.retrec.2012.06.006
25. Clifton, G.T., Mulley, C., Hensher, D.A.: Bus Rapid Transit versus Heavy Rail in suburban Sydney comparing successive iterations of a proposed heavy rail line project to the pre-existing BRT network. Res. Transp. Econ. **48**, 126–141 (2014)
26. Currie, G., Delbose, A.: Assessing Bus Rapid Transit system performance in Australasia. Res. Transp. Econ. **48**, 142–151 (2014)
27. Lin, Z., Wu, J.: Summary of the application effect of Bus Rapid Transit at Beijing south-centre corridor of China. J. Transp. Syst. Eng. Inf. Technol. **7**(4), 137–142 (2007)
28. Mejía-Dugand, S., Hjelm, O., Baas, L., Alberto, R.R.: Lessons from the spread of Bus Rapid Transit in Latin America. J. Clean. Prod. **50**, 82–90 (2014)
29. Muñoz, J.C., Batarce, M., Hidalgo, D.: Transantiago, five years after its launch. Res. Transp. Econ. **48**, 184–193 (2014)
30. Nuogoro, S.B., Fujiwara, A., Zhang, J.: The influence of BRT on the ambient PM10 concentration at roadside sites of Trans Jakarta Corridors. Procedia Environ. Sci. **2**, 914–924 (2010)
31. Rizvi, A., Sclar, E.: Implementing bus rapid transit: a tale of two Indian cities. Res. Transp. Econ. **48**, 194–204 (2014)
32. Tao, S., Corcoran, J., Mateo-Babiano, I., Rohde, D.: Exploring Bus Rapid Transit passenger travel behavior using big data. Appl. Geogr. **53**, 90–104 (2015)
33. Tiracini, A.: The economics and engineering of bus stops: spacing, design and congestion. Transp. Res. A **59**, 37–57 (2014)
34. Wöhrnschimmel, H., et al.: The impact of Bus Rapid Transit on commuter's exposure to Benzene, CO, PM2.5 and PN10 in Mexico City. Atmos. Environ. **42**, 8194–8203 (2008)
35. Wright, L., Hook, W.: Bus Rapid Transit Planning Guide. Institute for Transportation & Development Policy, New York, USA (2007)
36. Yazici, M., Levinson, H., Ilicalli, M., Camkasen, N., Kamga, C.: A bus rapid transit line case study: Istanbul's Metrobus System. J. Public Transp. **16**(1), 153–177 (2013)
37. Ji, J., Jou, J.: Forecast on bus trip demand based on ARIMA models and gated recurrent unit neural networks. In: 2017 International Conference on Computer Systems, Electronics and Control (ICCSEC), pp 105–108. IEEE (2017)
38. Gallo, M., De Luca, G., D'Acierno, L., Bottle, M.: Artificial neural networks for forecasting passenger flows on metro lines. Sensors J. **19**, 3424 1–14. https://doi.org/10.3390/s19153424
39. Gao, H., Xu, J., Li, S., Xu, L.: Forecast of passenger flow under the interruption of urban rail transit operation. In: Qin, Y., Jia, L., Liu, B., Liu, Z., Diao, L., An, M. (eds.) EITRT 2019. LNEE, vol. 639, pp. 283–291. Springer, Singapore (2020). https://doi.org/10.1007/978-981-15-2866-8_27
40. Chupin, A.L., Chupina, S., Morozova, N.: Prediction model of the efficacy and the implementation time of transportation intelligent systems. IOP Conf. Ser. Mater. Sci. Eng. **828**, 012006 (2019). IOP Publishing. https://doi.org/10.1088/1757-899x/828/1/012006

Mapping Biogas from Municipal Waste as Potential Clean Energy Areas in Central Mexico, Using Geographic Information Systems

Karen L. Carranco S.[1] , Sylvie J. Turpin-Marion[1] ,
and Diana G. Castro-Frontana[2(✉)]

[1] UAM-Azcapotzalco, Av. San Pablo 180. Col. Reynosa Tamaulipas, Ciudad de México, Mexico
[2] IPN-ENCB, Av. Wilfrido Massieu s/n, Col. UP. Adolfo López Mateos,
Ciudad de México, Mexico
dgcastro@ipn.mx

Abstract. Waste-to-energy (WtE) plants are management facilities that burn waste to produce electricity. Biogas plants are one form of WtE options. A prospective model to estimate biogas from solid waste was developed, combining two methodologies: Tchobanoglous and collaborators and the EPA-1996s equation. The first one uses urban solid waste composition to estimate biogas, while the later one converts biogas flow data into energy units (Mega-watts, MW). The resulting model is capable of estimating biogas from waste composition within any municipality in the study area (Mexico City, State of Mexico, Morelos, Puebla, and Querétaro) and it is also able to translate the potential biogas flow (in thousands of m^3/day) into megawatts (MW). A GIS was used to create choropleth maps representing the biogas volume that can be potentially produced in each region. The results obtained show that the Iztapalapa delegation in Mexico City could generate 62.63 MW. The Chimalhuacán region could reach 46 MW as well as some areas in Morelos. The use of solid waste in the Sierra Norte de Puebla was estimated in an energy capacity of 49.41 MW and finally, the Bajío Queretano obtained 37.83 MW. The GIS-location model was conceived for its use in prospective studies to locate potential WtE projects. The calculated energy from urban solid waste is presented in the form of graphs and maps, thus reflecting which region has a better potentiality for using this type of clean energy. This information is an important foundation for further spatial analyses using GIS and decision making.

Keywords: GIS · Biogas · Municipalities

1 Introduction

Waste generation within a place depends on multiple variables such as location, socioeconomic level, attitudes, and culture. In Mexico, between 1950 and 2017, the per capita generation went from 300 to 994 g per inhabitant per day. The State of Mexico along with Mexico City have the largest waste generation in the country, reflecting 16% and 12%

© Springer Nature Switzerland AG 2020
M. F. Mata-Rivera et al. (Eds.): GIS LATAM 2020, CCIS 1276, pp. 106–124, 2020.
https://doi.org/10.1007/978-3-030-59872-3_8

respectively of the national total, which for 2017 has been estimated at 120,128 t/day [1].

From the total municipal waste generated in Mexico, half of it corresponds to organic compounds (46.42%) [1] whose decomposition can be used to generate compost (via aerobic decomposition) or biomethane (via anaerobic decomposition) either in sanitary landfills or in facilities created for this purpose (WtE facilities). Waste-to-energy (WtE) plants are management facilities that burn waste to produce electricity. Biogas plants are one form of WtE options [2, 3].

Biogas is made up of approximately 50% methane (CH_4) and 50% carbon dioxide (CO_2), both of which are known as greenhouse gases (GHG), with methane being 24.5 times more contributing to the greenhouse effect than carbon dioxide [4]. Methane has a high energy content and is capable of being captured and used as a renewable energy source [2, 3]. Furthermore, methane represents a risk due to its high calorific value and its flammability, therefore it is not recommended that it be produced and emitted to the atmosphere under uncontrolled conditions [5].

In Mexico, the most used method for waste disposal is the sanitary landfill (as the best option) and open dumps (as the worst) [1]. A decomposition process of organic waste also occurs within sanitary landfills due to the environmental conditions created by the temperature, the presence or not of oxygen, the waste characteristics, and the age of the sanitary landfill. All this leads to a series of products, where liquid waste, better known as leachate, and gases such as biogas stand out [5].

Nowadays, several countries in the world, use biogas to generate energy, Europe is the world leader in biogas electricity production, with more than 10 GW installed and a number of 17,400 biogas plants [6]. As for Mexico, it uses only 2.4% of the biogas generated in landfills, since we lack the necessary infrastructure for its collection, or because there is not enough capacity for its economically viable exploitation [7, 8].

Many biogas projects from municipal waste to generate energy, have not been adequately developed in the country, due to multiple factors such as lack of planning, lack of financing, or lack of government support. Geographic Information Systems (GIS) can be used to generate prospective information. In this case, as for the potential biogas from waste that can be produced in a place and obtain technical data for feasibility projects. This would also allow us to comply with the obligations that Mexico has signed (regarding greenhouse gas emissions).

In the first part of this project, a prospective biogas model was developed from the composition of municipal waste to identify those areas that could have a high potential for its use as a clean energy option. In the second part, the results obtained from the model were combined with geo-referenced information on the location of municipalities, and a GIS that shows the results obtained through choropleth maps. In the third (and future) part of this project, the aim is to use the powerful tools of GIS to make spatial analyzes that allow finding the optimal location of future waste treatment facilities for their conversion into energy, looking for generating inter-municipal associations to make them environmentally friendly; technically viable and economically feasible.

This article focuses on the second phase of the project: the combination of the model results, with geospatial data, and the construction of maps.

2 State of the Art

As an introduction and to give an idea of how the results of the model were obtained, a brief explanation of the two models used for making up the prospective biogas model is presented.

2.1 Biogas Models in Sanitary Landfills

Numerous mathematical models allow for the estimation of potential biogas from waste. They also serve to assess potential risks associated with explosions and fires. Biogas models can also be used to evaluate project feasibility [4, 9–14].

Each model has its parameters, however, the amount of degradable waste deposited in sanitary landfills is considered a constant parameter among all of them. The most widely used models in Mexico are presented below.

The Tchobanoglous et al. Model

The Tchobanoglous and collaborators method involves the anaerobic digestion process that takes place in the organic fraction of waste, where its predominant products are carbon dioxide and methane, the main components of biogas. The organic fraction is divided into two classifications: 1) those residues that decompose rapidly (three months to five years) identified as RDS and 2) the residues that decompose slowly (up to 50 years or more) identified as SDS. This model requires knowing the elemental chemical composition of the waste (carbon [C], hydrogen [H], oxygen [O], and nitrogen [N]) [5]. The volume of gases emitted during the anaerobic decomposition can be represented by Eq. 1:

$$C_aH_bO_cN_d + \left(\frac{4a-b-2c+3d}{4}\right)H_2O \rightarrow \left(\frac{4a+b-2c-3d}{8}\right)CH_4 + \left(\frac{4a-b+2c+3d}{8}\right)CO_2 + dNH_3 \quad (1)$$

This model uses waste generation and waste composition data of each sub-product, the moisture content and dry weight to obtain the percentages of carbon, hydrogen, oxygen, nitrogen, sulfur, and ash from the waste. Having this composition and using the molecular weights of each chemical element, the waste chemical formula is obtained [identified as CHON]. Subsequently, from the chemical formula, the volumes of methane and carbon dioxide are estimated with the help of the specific weights of each compound. This methodology estimates the theoretical total amount of biogas that could be produced from the organic fraction of waste.

The LandGEM Model

Before the LandGEM model, the US Environmental Protection Agency (USEPA) published in the "Landfill Gas-to-Energy Project Development Manual" [15], an equation that correlates the potential for electrical energy to the biogas volume obtained from municipal waste decomposition. At the same time this equation sets the energy content of the biogas as a constant of approximately 500 Btu/ft3, and the heat rate for combustion engines in 12,000 Btu/kW, concluding in Eq. 2:

$$kW = \text{biogas flow}\left(\frac{ft^3}{day}\right) * \text{energy content}\left(\frac{Btu}{ft^3}\right) * \frac{1}{\text{heat rate}}\left(\frac{Btu}{kW}\right) * \frac{1\ day}{24\ hours}$$

$$(2)$$

Where:

kW = Gross power generation potential

Biogas flow = ft^3 of biogas obtained using the Tchobanoglous et al., method.

Energy content = the energy content of biogas (approximately 500 Btu/ft^3)

Heat rate of biogas for internal combustion engines = 12,000 Btu/kW

Later in 2001, the LandGEM model was created [16], which determines the volume of methane generated, using the potential for methane generation and the mass of deposited residues, mathematically described as shown in Eq. 3:

$$Q_{CH4} = \sum_{I=1}^{n} k(Lo)(Mi)\left(e^{-kt}\right) \tag{3}$$

Where:

Q_{CH4} = Methane emission rate [$m^3 CH_4$/t]

k = methane generation constant [t − 1]

Lo = methane generation potential [$m^3 CH_4$/kg waste]

Mi = mass of residues in the i-th section [mg]

t = time elapsed since the waste deposit (annual) [t]

At least 1 MW of electricity is expected to be generated within a sanitary landfill, to consider it useable for energy production [17, 18].

The Mexican Biogas Model

The Landfill Methane Outreach Program (LMOP) together with the United States Environmental Protection Agency (EPA) and other government agencies, developed the first Mexican Biogas model, to help operators and owners of landfills evaluate the importance and viability of capturing biogas and use it energetically [13]. This new version of the model uses a first-degree degradation equation. The following information is required for the estimation of biogas:

- Year of opening.
- Year of closure.
- Annual provisions.
- The annual average rainfall.
- Efficiency of the biogas collection system.

The last two biogas estimation models are more complicated to apply to landfills in Mexico since, currently, most of the parameters are difficult to obtain and there is no assurance of their veracity. Besides, these are applied to landfills that have a minimum operating period of one year.

There are other mathematical models, but this paper is not intended to explain the intricated details of the biogas-model created for this project but to present the biogas and potential energy maps obtained. However, it is important to highlight that, currently, no model uses waste data prospectively (as a decision-making tool where no landfills or WtE facilities exist). The one developed in the first part of this project does do that. It is also the first one that takes official information from State Waste Programs as input data.

2.2 Mapping Biogas Data

Montaño and collaborators established potential sites for biogas production in Mexico (Fig. 1). They determined that the minimum value for a place in the central zone of Mexico is 3 MW [19]. As a result of this research, and for the purpose of this study, it was established that the biogas generated by municipal waste is energetically usable from 3 MW on. This value is equivalent to 50,000 m^3 biogas per day.

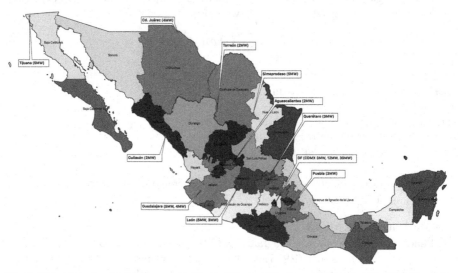

Fig. 1. Potential sites for biogas production in Mexico. Source: self elaboration from Montaño et al. (2009).

3 Methods

The biogas estimation model selected for this project was the one of Tchobanoglous and collaborators, since, as previously mentioned, it allows obtaining the volume of biogas generated by the organic fraction (rapid and slowly degradable), starting-off solely on the composition and amount of waste. This type of information is vital to analyze real biogas rates, from the first three months to five years to 50 years or more.

Subsequently, to obtain the results in energy terms, the EPA-1996 equation was used, which requires the volumetric flow of biogas to provide results in terms of mega-watts (MW).

3.1 Making up the Biogas Model (1st Phase of the Project)

The central area of the Mexican Republic was chosen, specifically the states of Mexico City, the State of Mexico, Morelos, Puebla, and Querétaro because of the following reasons:

1. Waste generation: Mexico City and the State of Mexico are the two states that generate the most municipal waste in the entire country.
2. Neighboring states: Mexico City has borders with the State of Mexico and Morelos. Hidalgo, Puebla, and Querétaro are also part of the central states which have a significant contribution to the national waste generation.
3. Potential energy capacity: according to the study made by Montaño and collaborators, Querétaro and Puebla stood out for their electrical energy capacity coming from landfill gases (Montaño).
4. Data availability: the five states considered in the study have in common the availability of waste composition data for the entire state (or most of their municipalities), which made it possible to generalize data to the model.

Once the selected models and the study area were analyzed, it was determined to generate two information forms, 1) a general information form (Table 1), and 2) a specific information form (on waste from any selected municipality) (Table 2). These forms were the basis for completing the data required by the biogas estimation model. That is, the data from the five states of the study area were unified using the arrangement shown in Table 1 and Table 2.

Table 1. Structure of the general information form

General information					
Municipality	ID (CVE_Mun)	State	State ID	Region	Population

Table 2. Specific waste information form (for any municipality within the study area)

RDS[1] Waste sub-product (composition) (tonnes/day)	SDS[2] waste sub-product (composition) (tonnes/day)
Organic (food) waste	Plastics
Paper	Glass (labels on glass)
Cardboard	Metals
Garden waste	Textiles
	Wood
	Disposable diapers

[1] RDS stands for "rapid degradability subproduct" (in waste)
[2] SDS stands for "slow degradability subproduct" (in waste)

- *Waste information*: All the information regarding waste composition was obtained from the latest official reports available for each state. Then, the information was categorized using the forms shown in Table 1 and Table 2. The data were processed using Microsoft Excel.

– *Biogas estimation:* The chemical formula of waste for any municipality is obtained using the Eq. 1. Then, the biogas is obtained using the method described by Tchobanoglous and collaborators [5].
– *Conversion to megawatts:* The biogas flow is converted to potential electricity using Eq. 2 and the method described by the EPA model [15].

3.2 Building the Biogas GIS (2st Phase of the Project)

The information from a total of 405 municipalities was processed and calculated by the Excel biogas model and the results were arranged in five categories:

– Waste generation (in tonnes/day)
– Biogas from RDS fraction (in thousand m^3/day)
– Biogas from the SDS fraction (in thousand m^3/day)
– Potential biogas generation (sum of RDS and SDS fractions) (in thousand m^3/day)
– Potential electricity generation from biogas (in megawatts MW)

Later, the information of the biogas-model was exported as independent csv files for each state.

Geodatabase: Vectorial layers (shapefiles) were obtained for the same municipalities. They were downloaded from the National Geostatistical Framework webpage. Shapefiles for each state (Mexico City, State of Mexico, Morelos, Queretaro, and Puebla) and its municipalities were obtained and depurated to preserve only the ID field (CVE_MUN), the state ID (CVE_ENT) and the municipality name field (NOM_MUN).

On the other hand, the cvs files exported from Excel were joined to their respective shapefiles (using the municipality ID as the common ID). This was done using the table union option in the software QGIS Pi.

Choropleth Maps Definition: After the shapefiles were joined to the CSV tables, new shapefiles were created for each state. A GIS project was made using the QGIS Pi software. Maps showing the biogas flow and the potential MW production were created by mapping the corresponding field on the attributes table of each state (V4 and V5). Graphs were also created showing the results for each municipality.

4 Results

The results obtained from the biogas model were classified in a database for each Mexican state using the following codes (Table 3):

Each municipality has a unique code assigned by the National Institute of Statistics, Geography and Informatics (INEGI). Therefore, the database was constructed using the geo-code of each municipality as its exclusive ID (CVE_MUN) and then each field on the table corresponds to a result from the biogas model (as previously indicated in Table 3). At the same time, each state is divided into different regions (according to their official state programs) to facilitate environmental management, including waste

Table 3. Codes to identify the results from the biogas model.

Waste generation (tonnes/day)	V1
Biogas from RDS fraction (thousand m3/day)	V2
Biogas from SDS fraction (thousand m3/day)	V3
Potential biogas generation (thousand m3/day)	V4
Potential electricity generation from biogas (MW)	V5

management issues. These regions were considered for arranging the information in the database since it is important to consider neighborhood properties for future spatial analysis. For example, two or more municipalities with low biogas potential can unite in the same project and make energy from biogas feasible for all of them if they find the best location for a WtE facility).

4.1 Geodatabase Structure

The following figures show the results of every municipality for three of the states within the study area in the following order: Mexico City (Table 4), Morelos (Table 5)

Table 4. Mexico City's waste generation, biogas and potential electricity results.

CVE_MUN	V1	V2	V3	V4	V5
010	665.00	154.56	290.11	444.67	28.59
002	507.00	146.08	140.29	286.36	18.41
014	699.00	172.48	189.92	362.40	23.30
003	795.00	185.02	228.75	413.77	26.61
004	183.00				
015	1293.00	433.72	335.09	768.81	49.43
005	1704.00	464.24	477.83	942.07	60.58
006	472.00				0.00
007	2272.00	594.27	379.74	974.01	62.63
008	257.00				
016	812.00	198.32	219.51	417.83	26.87
009	118.00	29.71	36.03	65.74	4.23
011	351.00				
012	853.00	178.82	312.82	491.64	31.61
017	842.00	213.29	264.05	477.34	30.69
013	435.00	110.45	134.35	244.79	15.74

Table 5. Morelos' waste generation, biogas and potential electricity results.

CV_MUN	V1	V2	V3	V4	V5
007	553.03	126.63	237.82	364.45	23.43
008	79.922	18.30	34.37	52.67	3.39
011	279.26	63.95	120.09	184.03	11.83
018	114.07	26.12	49.05	75.17	4.83
028	59.96	13.73	25.78	39.51	2.54
002	8.974	1.75	5.46	7.21	0.46
016	7.876	1.54	4.79	6.33	0.41
022	9.159	1.79	5.57	7.36	0.47
030	26.797	5.23	16.30	21.53	1.38
005	5.67	1.03	3.83	4.87	0.31
014	7.27	2.12	1.77	3.89	0.25
015	14.79	2.69	10.00	12.69	0.82
021	4.76	0.86	3.22	4.08	0.26
004	64.9	11.57	43.26	54.82	3.53
020	47	8.38	31.33	39.70	2.55
029	124.5	22.19	82.98	105.17	6.76
003	21.95	5.24	8.92	14.16	0.91
010	8.75	2.09	3.55	5.64	0.36
013	7.23	1.73	2.94	4.66	0.30
033	6.57	1.57	2.67	4.24	0.27
019	17.47	4.17	7.10	11.27	0.72
032	4	0.95	1.62	2.58	0.17
023	3.56	0.71	1.92	2.63	0.17
026	12.41	2.47	6.68	9.15	0.59
027	8.2	1.63	4.41	6.05	0.39
001	9.43	2.02	3.82	5.84	0.38
012	36.91	7.89	14.97	22.86	1.47
017	44.73	9.57	18.14	27.70	1.78
024	15.51	3.32	6.29	9.61	0.62
025	22.85	4.89	9.26	14.15	0.91
031	25.33	5.42	10.27	15.69	1.01
006	226.67	52.57	75.94	128.52	8.26
009	12.26	2.24	7.79	10.04	0.65

and Queretaro (Table 6). The municipalities geo-codes in all tables are not shown in numerical order but alphabetical order instead, according to the region they belong to.

The results for the State of Mexico and Puebla are not shown here because these two states have more than 150 municipalities each and that makes their tables very large.

Table 6. Querétaro's waste generation, biogas and potential electricity results.

CV_MUN	V1	V2	V3	V4	V5
014	789.72	193.14	316.43	509.57	32.77
006	123.01	30.07	48.64	78.71	5.06
001	30.02	7.34	11.86	19.20	1.23
008	12.98	3.17	5.13	8.30	0.53
011	119.94	29.33	47.37	76.70	4.93
012	42.97	10.51	16.98	27.49	1.77
016	188.94	46.21	74.63	120.85	7.77
017	47.98	11.74	18.95	30.69	1.97
007	40.99	10.02	16.20	26.22	1.69
004	40	9.78	15.79	25.57	1.64
005	44.98	11.00	17.76	28.76	1.85
013	17.01	4.15	6.73	10.88	0.70
018	15.99	3.92	6.32	10.23	0.66
002	10.476	2.69	4.32	7.01	0.45
003	10.02	2.45	3.95	6.40	0.41
009	15.99	3.92	6.32	10.23	0.66
015	5.52	1.22	1.97	3.19	0.20
010	14.99	3.67	5.91	9.59	0.62

4.2 Biogas Choropleth Maps

The GIS-location model was conceived for its use in prospective studies to locate potential WtE projects. The calculated biogas flow from urban solid waste is presented in the form of graphs and choropleth maps for all the states included in the study area (Figs. 2, 3, 4, 5, and 6):

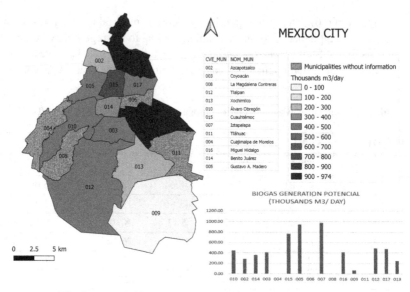

Fig. 2. Potential biogas flow within Mexico City municipalities.

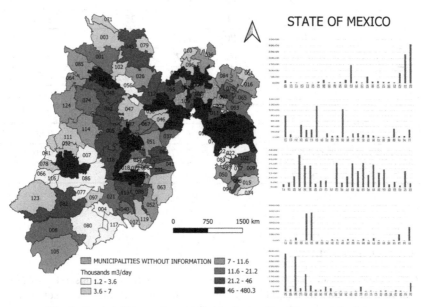

Fig. 3. Potential biogas flow within the State of Mexico municipalities.

The largest generation of biogas comes from the municipalities of Iztapalapa (CVE_MUN 007) with 974 thousand m³/day and Gustavo A. Madero (CVE_MUN 005) with 942 thousand m³/day. This generation is directly related to the population since Iztapalapa is the most populous, followed by Gustavo A. Madero, a pattern that is constant for any state. Together they represent 32.54% of the biogas emission in the whole Mexico City. However, it is important to mention that, in demographic terms, they are in fourth place with 117 km^2, and in sixth place with 94 km^2, respectively.

This means that high populated areas represent a serious problem for waste management and the location of any waste management facility.

For the State of Mexico, the municipalities with the highest biogas flows are Nezahualcóyotl (CVE_MUN 058) with 480 thousand m^3/day, followed by Naucalpan de Juárez (CVE_MUN 057) with 463 thousand m^3/day.

In turn, the municipalities of Valle de Chalco Solidaridad, Atlacomulco, Chicoloapan Chimalhuacán, Ixtapaluca, La Paz, Ecatepec, Nicolás Romero, Texcoco, Atizapán de Zaragoza, Tlalnepantla de Baz, Toluca, Coacalco de Berriozábal, Cuautitlán and Zumpango within, generate bio range from 100 to 300 thousand m^3/day. On the other hand, despite the fact that municipalities below the value of 50 thousand m^3 of biogas per day dominate, the inter-municipality concept would offer a solution for the efficient use of waste (instead of landfilling).

It is important to note that Mexico City and the State of Mexico together account for 28% of waste generation in the country [1]. This means that the potential for a feasible WtE project within this area is high. As a matter of fact, Mexico City had already made a licitation for a WtE project in 2017–2018. Unfortunately, it was cancelled due to political reasons. Mexico City, being the capital of the country, does not have any landfill within its territory and its waste is sent to the State of Mexico and Morelos [20].

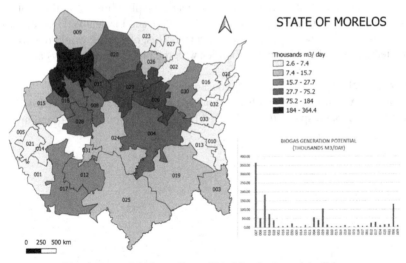

Fig. 4. Potential biogas flow within Morelos' municipalities.

In Morelos the municipalities with the highest biogas flows are Jiutepec (CVE_MUN 011) with 184 thousand m^3/day, Yautepec (CVE_MUN 029) with 105 thousand m^3/day, and Temixco (CVE_MUN 018) with 75 thousand m^3/day.

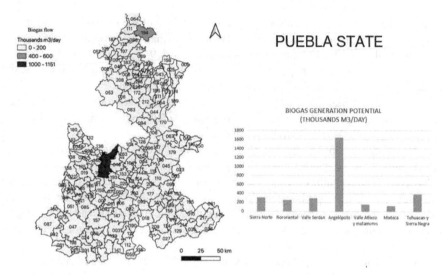

Fig. 5. Potential biogas flow within Puebla municipalities.

Puebla represents the largest territory with 33,919 km^2 and 217 municipalities. It is important to note that, as shown in the cartographic representation, most of the municipalities barely exceed 12 thousand m^3 per day of biogas, which is considered a non-feasible value for WtE projects. However, this state is a clear example of the possibility that "low-biogas municipalities" might come together, to sum up, and locale a WtE facility where neighbors towns can benefit from the same project. This, of course, would require more detailed technical studies. The municipalities with the highest biogas-flows are:

- Amozoc (CVE_MUN 015) with 69 thousand m^3/day,
- Tehuacán (CVE_MUN 156) with 182 thousand m^3/day and
- The city of Puebla (capital) (CVE_MUN 114) with 1 million 151 thousand m^3/day.

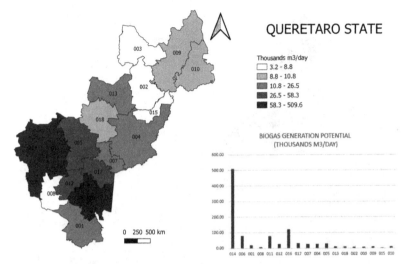

Fig. 6. Potential biogas flow within Querétaro municipalities.

The state of Querétaro has the lowest values of biogas compared to other states in the study area. Most of its municipalities are in the range of 3,000 m³ per day up to 30,000 m³ of biogas per day.

The municipalities with the highest biogas flows are Querétaro (CVE_MUN 014) with 509 thousand m³/day, San Juan del Río (CVE_MUN 016) with 120 thousand m³/day; Corregidora (CVE_MUN 006), with 78 thousand m³/day and El Marqués (CVE_MUN 011) with 76 thousand and m³/day. The choropleth map reflects that the largest generation of biogas occurs in the southern part of the state. This information is key for the possible construction of an interstate facility in association with the State of Mexico.

4.3 Potential Electricity Generation from Biogas

The following figures (Fig. 7, 8, 9 and 10) show the results in potential megawatts obtained from biogas. Each municipality is now labeled with the field V5 (MW) instead of the municipality ID (CVE_MUN). Each municipality has a unique calculated value in MW. Even when a municipality might have less than 3 MW potential, this does not mean that it is out of a WtE project. What we want to explore with future spatial analyses are pre-feasibility scenarios where two or more neighbor municipalities can join together to explore inter-municipal WtE projects. Spatial analyses can also be useful to find the best location for a WtE project considering other geographic aspects such as topography, travel time, costs, etc.

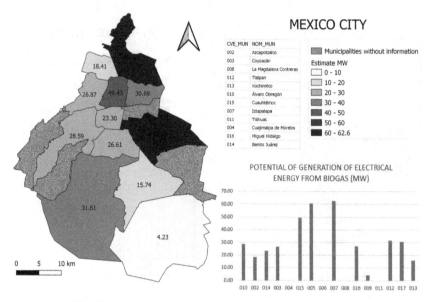

Fig. 7. Potential MW production from biogas in Mexico City.

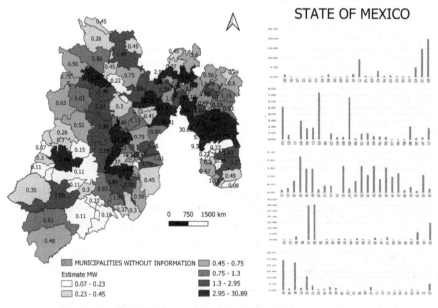

Fig. 8. Potential MW generation from biogas in the State of Mexico.

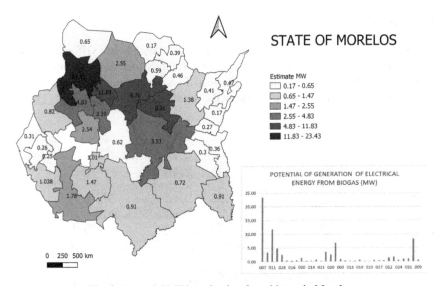

Fig. 9. Potential MW production from biogas in Morelos.

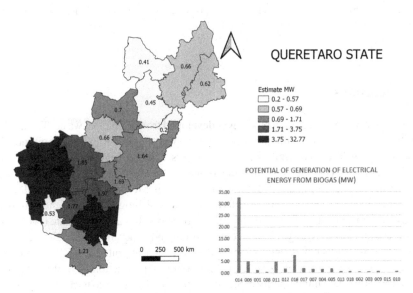

Fig. 10. Potential MW production from biogas in Querétaro.

4.4 Future Research

The next part of this project consists of having the data onto a web GIS platform and create additional layers of information to perform future spatial analyses and to make the information available for public use. The shapefiles were uploaded onto the ArcGIS online platform to show an example on how the results would look like (Fig. 11):

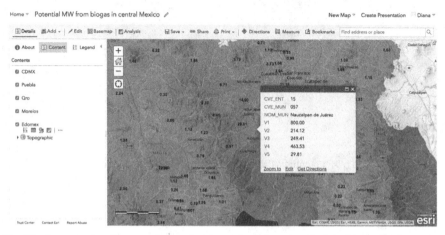

Fig. 11. An example of how can layers showing potential megawatts from biogas be shown on a web GIS platform.

5 Conclusions

A prospective biogas calculation model was developed from municipal waste. The model, identified as the "Biogas-estimation model for central states of Mexico", combines the methodology of Tchobanoglous and collaborators and the EPA 1996 equation. The resulting model is capable of estimating biogas from waste composition within any municipality in the study area (Mexico City, State of Mexico, Morelos, Puebla, and Querétaro) and it is also able to translate the potential biogas flow (in thousands of m^3/day) into megawatts (MW). This model can be applied in any other state (even from another country) as long as waste data composition and generation are available.

The biogas results calculated by the model were later migrated to a GIS project and several maps were created showing the potential biogas production as well as potential electricity within each municipality in the study area. A GIS was used to create choropleth maps representing the biogas volume that can be potentially produced in each region.

The results obtained show that the Iztapalapa delegation in Mexico City could generate 62.63 MW. The Chimalhuacán region could reach 46 MW as well as some areas in Morelos. The use of solid waste in the Sierra Norte de Puebla was estimated in an energy capacity of 49.41 MW and finally, the Bajío queretano obtained 37.83 MW.

The next phase of this study will include having the biogas and potential energy results available onto a GIS web platform for performing spatial analyses to find potential best locations for inter-municipal WtE projects.

Acknowledgments. The authors of this work thank the National Polytechnic Institute, COFAA, and the Autonomous Metropolitan University for their support in carrying out and presenting this project.

References

1. SEMARNAT-Secretaría de Medio Ambiente y Recursos Naturales: Diagnóstico básico para la gestión integral de los residuos. SEMARNAT, Mexico (2020). https://www.gob.mx/cms/uploads/attachment/file/555093/DiagnosticoBasicoGestionIntegralResiduosF.pdf.pdf. Accessed 20 Jul 2020
2. GIZ-Deutsche Gesellschaft für Internationale Zusammenarbei: Waste-to-Energy options in municipal solid waste management. GIZ, Germany (2017). https://www.giz.de/en/downloads/GIZ_WasteToEnergy_Guidelines_2017.pdf. Accessed 20 Jul 2020
3. Ullah Khan, I., et al.: Biogas as a renewable energy fuel – a review of biogas upgrading, utilisation and storage. Energy Convers. Manage. **150**, 277–294 (2017)
4. Eggleston, H.S., Buendia, L., Miwa, K., Ngara, T., Tanabe, K. (eds.): IPCC Guidelines for National Greenhouse Gas Inventories, Volume 5 – Waste. Prepared by the National Greenhouse Gas Inventories Programme. IGES, Japan (2006)
5. Tchobanoglous, G., Theisen, H., Viguil, S.A.: Integrated Solid Waste Management: Engineering Principles and Management Issues. Mc. Graw-Hill, United States (1993)
6. Scarlat, N., Dallemand, J.F., Fahl, F.: Biogas: Developments and perspectives in Europe. Renew. Energy **129**, 457–472 (2018)
7. Castro, G.A.: México aprovecha sólo el 2.4 por ciento del biogás potencial de rellenos sanitarios. UNAM Bull. Mex. (2013). http://www.dgcs.unam.mx/boletin/bdboletin/2013_005.html. Accessed 12 Feb 2017
8. Díaz, I., Domínguez, A., Barredo, I.: Nuevos retos en el tratamiento de residuos. Revista Técnica de Medio Ambiente **169**, 32–36 (2013)
9. Córdoba, V., Blanco, G., Santalla, E.: Modelado de la generación de biogás en rellenos sanitarios. Revista Avances en Energías Renovables y Medio Ambiente **13** 06.69–06.76 (2009)
10. Machado, S.L., Carvalho, M.F., Gourc, J.-P., Vilar, O.M., do Nascimento, J.C.: Methane generation in tropical landfills: simplified methods and field results. Waste Manage. **29**(1), 153–161 (2009)
11. Breno, C.D., Ramos, J.R., de Sousa Silva, R., Cattanio, J.H., do Couto, L.L., Mitschein, T.A.: Estimates of methane emissions and comparison with gas mass burned in CDM action in a large landfill in Eastern Amazon. Waste Manage. **101**, 28–34 (2020)
12. Spokas, K., et al.: Methane mass balance at three landfill sites: what is the efficiency of capture by gas collection systems? Waste Manage. **26**, 516–525 (2006)
13. Aguilar-Virgen, Q., Taboada-González, P.A., Ojeda-Benítez, S.: Modelo mexicano para la estimación de la generación de biogás. Ingeniería-Revista Académica de la Facultad de Ingeniería, Universidad Autónoma de Yucatán **15**(1), 37–45 (2011)
14. Lima, R.M., et al.: Spatially distributed potential of landfill biogas production and electric power generation in Brazil. Waste Manage. **74**, 323–334 (2018)
15. United States EPA-Environmental Protection Agency: Turning a Liability into an Asset: A Landfill Gas-to-Energy Project Development Handbook. Report no. EPA 430-B-96-0004 (1996)

16. EPA-Environmental Protection Agency: Volume III Landfilling (2001). https://www.epa.gov/sites/production/files/2015-08/documents/iii15_apr2001.pdf. Accessed 20 Jul 2020
17. Arvizu F.J.: Evaluación del potencial energético de los rellenos sanitarios. Revista AIDIS de Ingeniería y Ciencias Ambientales: Investigación, desarrollo y práctica 1(1), 1–14 (2006)
18. Arvizu F.J.: La basura como recurso energético situación actual y prospectiva de México. Revista de Ingeniería Civil 496, 1–9 (2010)
19. Montaño, O.A., Corona, A.J., Montelongo, R.M.: Metodología sistémica para el desarrollo de un proyecto de Biogás. XIII Congreso Internacional de Investigación en Ciencias Administrativas. La administración frente a la globalización: Gobernabilidad y desarrollo (2009)
20. SEDEMA-Secretaría del Medio Ambiente del Gobierno de la Ciudad de México: Inventario de Residuos Sólidos de la Ciudad de México 2018. SEDEMA, Mexico (2019)

Geographic Information Systems for Forest Species Distribution and Habitat Suitability

Angélica Navarro-Martínez[1]($\boxtimes$) ⓘ, Gregorio Ramírez-Magil[2] ⓘ,
and Martín A. Mendoza B.[3] ⓘ

[1] El Colegio de la Frontera Sur, Chetumal, Quintana Roo, Mexico
manava@ecosur.mx
[2] Fomento al Desarrollo Social y Manejo de Vida Silvestre, A.C., Chetumal,
Quintana Roo, Mexico
shedaia@hotmail.com
[3] Colegio de Postgraduados, Veracruz, Veracruz, Mexico
mmendoza@colpos.mx

Abstract. The reach and descriptive capabilities of geographic information systems are displayed using a pair of examples modeling distribution range and habitat suitability for big-leaf mahogany *Swietenia macrophylla* King from the Yucatan Peninsula of Mexico based on the National Forest and Soils Inventory database. Big-leaf mahogany is an economically important species in the Neotropics. For over three centuries, it has been selectively extracted from tropical forest, threatening its populations. These examples show that this region contains, and it will continue to hold large areas suitable for big-leaf mahogany. Although models predict a decrease in the extent of the regional big-leaf mahogany natural distribution, suitable habitat is expected to be abundant in Quintana Roo, Mexico. These studies have taken full advantage of GIS capabilities to integrate georeferenced data with explanatory environmental factors. Models of these relationships have turned out to be effective tools that generate valuable information for decision making and scientific understanding of the issues and concerns regarding big-leaf mahogany.

Keywords: Big-leaf mahogany · MaxEnt · Species distribution model (SDM)

1 Introduction

Geographic information systems (GIS) comprise a category of software tools with ample usage potential for managing spatially explicit data. GIS applications provide means to display species distribution ranges and suitability habitat for valuable timber species such as big- leaf mahogany *Swietenia macrophylla* King [1]. Species distribution and suitability habitat are two issues that can be addressed as mathematical models that relate locations where the species occurs

© Springer Nature Switzerland AG 2020
M. F. Mata-Rivera et al. (Eds.): GIS LATAM 2020, CCIS 1276, pp. 125–135, 2020.
https://doi.org/10.1007/978-3-030-59872-3_9

to environmental features in those places. GIS software such as ArcGIS, ArcMap, QGIS, DIVA-GIS, and gvSIG make it possible to integrate species distribution with ecological factors (climate, soil, land use) [2]. Recent GIS applications that portray species distribution include Navarro-Martínez et al., in 2018. On the other hand, a habitat suitability model was developed by Ramírez et al. (in press). GIS models are built on two tiers: 1. Primary data on species presence as shown in forest inventories and herbarium metadata, and 2. Secondary data about climate and physical environment (soil, topography and such). Secondary data usually comes from repositories such as WorldClim[1] [3]. WorldClim offers global climatic data with a one-kilometer spatial resolution at the Equator. Other data sources for Mexico include Instituto Nacional de Estadística y Geografia (INEGI)[2], Comisión Nacional para el Conocimiento y Uso de la Biodiversidad (CONABIO)[3], and Comisión Nacional Forestal (CONAFOR)[4].

The two models presented here will showcase the reach and modeling capabilities of GIS. The cases model big-leaf mahogany distribution and habitat suitability. Big leaf mahogany is a highly appreciated fine timber that is an economically important and emblematic of the Neotropics. This species grows as an emerging tree in humid and dry forests of diverse soil and climate characteristics [4–6]. Big-leaf mahogany also grows among secondary vegetation after catastrophic disturbances and after traditional Maya slash and burn agriculture [7–9].

The natural distribution of big-leaf mahogany covers around 8 000 km^2, encompassing from southern Mexico down to the northern regions of Brazil and Bolivia [10]. Lamb in 1966 considers that the best big-leaf mahogany is the one from tropical dry forests [11]. In Mexico, big-leaf mahogany is found in six southeastern states [12]. One of the largest Mexican populations is the one in the Yucatan Peninsula [13]. This population is considered one of the best remaining in Mexico (Fig. 1). On the Yucatan Peninsula, many forest communities depend on big-leaf mahogany harvests to obtain suitable profits from their forest management operations [14].

Historic records of big-leaf mahogany logging span for over three centuries [15–17]. Current forest structure is dominated by juvenile pole size trees in dense stands, old growth and regeneration spots are rare [18]. However, land development and commercial logging in the Yucatan Peninsula for the last twenty years appear to have not encroached on the natural mahogany forests, as they have in other regions [1].

Currently, big-leaf mahogany is listed in Mexico as vulnerable and prone to extinction [19–21]. Since 1998 big-leaf mahogany was labeled as vulnerable in the CITES list of endangered internationally traded species [22]. It was known that at the end of the 20th Century mahogany was present in an estimated 36% of its potential area [23]. In the case of Mexico, the loss of mahogany forests

---

[1] http://www.worldclim.org/.

[2] https://www.inegi.org.mx.

[3] https://www.gob.mx/conabio.

[4] https://www.gob.mx/conafor.

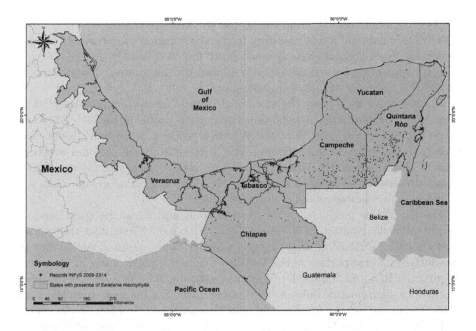

Fig. 1. Field reports of presence of big-leaf mahogany (*Swietenia macrophylla*) King in Mexico. Source: National Forest and Soils Inventory database.

adds up to an estimated 76% [24]. As a caveat, it should be stated that some researchers consider these figures speculative [25].

An array of modeling approaches has been developed to link bioclimatic variables to the presence of species on the ground. Most models assume that climate regulates the distribution of species [26,27]. These models make it possible to forecast changes in the future distribution of diverse species and ecosystems [28–33]. This paper presents the results of two studies that model potential distribution and habitat suitability of *Swietenia macrophylla* King in the Yucatan Peninsula of Mexico. These models convey ecological information for the management of this species and its habitat, since mahogany is associated to over 200 other tree species and many other life forms.

2   Potential Distribution of Big-Leaf Mahogany in Mexico

In a previous study from 2018, a model was produced to represent the potential area of distribution of *S. macrophylla* (Fig. 2) [1]. This model was developed using MaxEnt version 3.3.3 [34]. Input data was made up of 393 field plots where the species was present based on the National Forest and Soils Inventory database (INFyS) in 2004–2009. Climatic variables were provided by WorldClim. Ancillary information was added to include vegetation and land use patterns. This explanatory information was provided by CONAFOR (scale 1:

250,000) [12]. INEGI's elevation model (30 by 30 m resolution) was also used. CONAFOR's national forest inventory in the study region comprises of 248 conglomerates. Each conglomerate is made up of four rectangular subplots 400 m^2 each. Conglomerates are systematically placed on the ground. These samples contain 566 instances of mahogany presence.

MaxEnt software follows the statistical concept of maximum entropy. The software allows estimates of potential distribution probabilities [35]. All coordinate values are coded as Mercator **WGS84** geodesic projection. Results are displayed using ArcGIS 9.2 software. The MaxEnt software provides an AUC value to assess the model. Model performance means efficacy in discriminating among sites with and without mahogany [36]. An AUC value greater than 0.5 indicates an acceptable model performance [34].

The Fig. 2 was produced by MaxEnt output, and it can be considered as the potential distribution of *S. macrophylla*. This model resembles the species known actual distribution (Fig. 1), except for an overly elevated probability in the south-southwest portion of the Yucatan Peninsula, particularly in the states of Quintana Roo and Campeche. This zone seems to have in a wide geographic area with a high-quality habitat. The model identifies the best conditions for mahogany in the largest forestry ejidos as Petcacab and Noh Bec in the center of the state and Tres Garantias and Caoba in the southern part of Quintana Roo. In Campeche, the best habitat for mahogany was found in the Calakmul region [1]. Community forestry has been developed in this area since the early 1980s, proving to be a good strategy for forest conservation [14].

The example model reached an AUC value of 0.9. Vegetation was the variable with the highest contribution to the model, and high and medium tropical forest covers were closely related. Vegetation was also important. A model for the same species in Veracruz, Mexico [37] arrived at the same outcome. Elevation too was an important factor. Climatic variables explained a minor part of the model projections.

3 Habitat Suitability of Big-Leaf Mahogany in Mexico

Distribution models can include trends of change in climatic variables [38–40]. This capability invites inquiries into the effect of the current problem of accelerated global climatic change. Effects of climatic change are expected to show as variations of forest structure and composition, as well as changes in species distribution patterns [41,42]. Models based upon the idea of habitat suitability have shown the likelihood of diminishing the range of distribution for some species. This topic has been addressed by several researchers [43–48]; their work improves the understanding of those changes, their size and trend [49].

Ramírez-Magil et al. in print used models to assess the habitat suitability distribution of *Swietenia macrophylla* King in the Yucatan Peninsula of Mexico, and to forecast future distribution under two scenarios of climatic change [50]. The second model in this paper drew its input data from INFyS 2009–2014, WorldClim, and CONABIO's biogeographic provinces [51]. Data was input into MaxEnt and ArcGIS for processing.

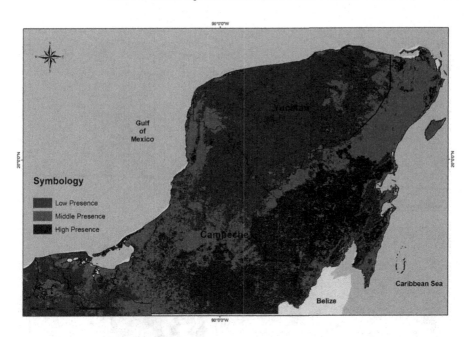

Fig. 2. Potential distribution of *Swietenia macrophylla* King in the Yucatan Peninsula, Mexico.

Raster files for each of 19 bio-climatic variables were produced for the study area using options in the environment settings menu of ArcMap 10.4.1. Raster data were trimmed using the extract by mask tool from the same software.

The resulting model (Fig. 3), used 270 locations of species reports (80%), soil type, and six bioclimatic variables as input for MaxEnt. The 20% of unused field registers were set apart for later use in independently validate the model. Validation was carried using Partial Roc software [52].

Future scenarios estimates required alternative climatic parameters. These were taken from the general circulation model MRI-CGCM3. This climate change model assumes that global emissions will peak in 2040. The rendering of projected scenarios was possible using ArcMap 10.4.1. In this process, maximum sensibility and specificity of 0.254, 0.238, 0.275 (2020, 2050, 2070, respectively), were the thresholds for reclassification of the species presence or absence. This screening produced a map for each scenario, and from them, it was possible to tally pixels that changed their value of presence or absence of mahogany. The tally was then converted to area estimates.

The resulting MaxEnt model exhibits a great influence of soil type (32.4%), precipitation season (14.7%), and diurnal temperature spread (8.5%). A total of 7 017 106.68 ha were deemed suitable habitat for *S. macrophylla* (Fig. 3A). Campeche (41%) and Quintana Roo (32%) were the states with the largest area suitable for mahogany. These figures are close to the current occupation area.

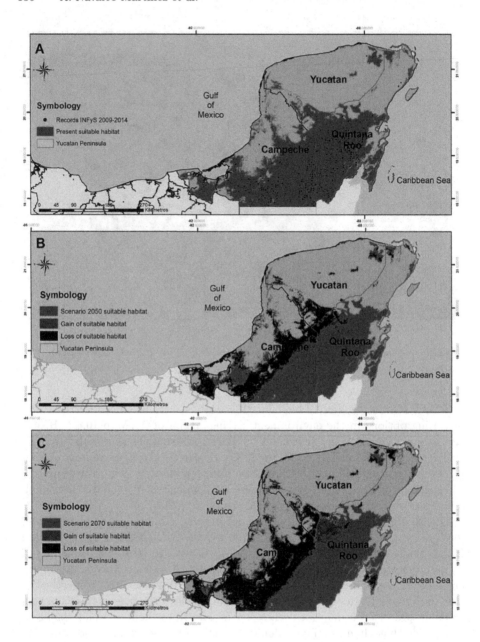

Fig. 3. Suitable habitat for *Swietenia macrophylla* King in the Yucatan Peninsula, Mexico.

Navarro-Martínez et al. in 2018 findings are about the same amount, hence suggesting that there is a significant area of mahogany habitat in the Yucatan Peninsula today (2020).

The 2050 scenario expects 4 714 137.45 ha of suitable habitat, this is equivalent to a 32.8% decline respect to 2020 (Fig. 3B). In this scenario, Campeche would still retain some 37% of lands with suitable habitat, while Quintana Roo would be holding 48.6% of the 2020 suitable habitat.

The expectation for the year 2070 is to have 3 964 615.11 ha, or a loss of 56.5% of the present habitat, equivalent to a 15.9% decrease relative to the 2050 scenario. At this later time, Quintana Roo will be highly relevant in preserving the species and its habitat in México (Fig. 3C).

The reduced suitable habitat expected in 2070 might be explained because of the emissions peak in 2040, and subsequent subsiding running up to 2070. Habitat suitability estimated for 2050 could be related to precipitation reductions and increases in temperature those years. The habitat losses could possibly be larger than expected according to Calvo y Rivera in 2000.

It is important to keep into perspective that Quintana Roo and Campeche hold today extensive mahogany populations, even though the species has been harvested for over 300 years. Current populations continue being logged because they are an important resource for Maya communities that practice their traditional management schemes of slash and burn. Traditional community forestry has shown to be successful in securing a continuous renovation of the forest within the constraints and goals of natural resources sustainable management.

4   Conclusion

The use of GIS and their supplementary software have shown effective modeling capabilities to study the distribution and suitability of mahogany habitat. These models generate visions of the future and elicit connections and explanations about the trends in species occupation. These insights are valuable when handed over those in charge of decisions, and they are also important in supporting scientific explanations of the species trends.

The potential distribution of *S. macrophylla* obtained from the MaxEnt software predicted the greatest probability of occurrence as wide and continuous expanses of habitat in the southern and southeastern regions of the Yucatan Peninsula. This outcome is consistent which field reports of presence, although its abundance varies. The spatial potential distribution model was best explained by vegetation cover (medium- and high-stature semievergreen tropical forest), and elevation. In this area are found today and for the future the most suitable habitat conditions for the permanence of the species, particularly in Quintana, which according to the projections of the MaxEnt model tested for the years 2050 and 2070, will conserve around 50% of the current area in the natural distribution range of the species in Mexico; although the general trend between the present scenarios, 2050 and 2070 is a decrease in habitat. This region represents one of the most important and continuous relics of tropical vegetation in Mexico, which implies a challenge for its permanence given the pressure on natural resources by land use change.

Nevertheless, the economic importance of *S. macrophylla*, current evidence suggests changing forest management at the guide species level to management of all species in the forest to favor their regeneration; also, silvicultural practices should be promoted that favor the rapid growth of seedlings and young individuals in such a way as to favor recruitment and with it, the recovery of harvested individuals.

5 Future Work

Given the importance of big-leaf mahogany in contributing to the economy of the families in the forest communities where it is distributed, it is necessary to complete the knowledge about its ecology by incorporating information about the demographic behavior of the species in the region, and that allows the elaboration of a robust proposal for the management and conservation of the species and the forests of Quintana Roo. This requires the design and establishment of a long-term monitoring network.

References

1. Navarro-Martínez, A., Ellis, E.A., Hernández-Gómez, I., Romero-Montero, J.A., Sánchez-Sánchez, O.: Distribution and abundance of big-leaf mahogany (Swietenia macrophylla) on the Yucatan Peninsula, Mexico. Trop. Conserv. Sci. **11**, 1–17 (2018). https://doi.org/10.1177/1940082918766875
2. Gastón-González, A.: Aplicación de los Sistemas de Información Geográfica a estudios florísticos y Corológicos: algunos ejemplos. Cuadernos de la Sociedad Española de Ciencias Forestales **28**, 9–13 (2008)
3. Hijmans, R.J., Cameron, S.E., Parra, J.L., Jones, P.G., Jarvis, A.: Very high-resolution interpolated climate surfaces for global land areas. Int. J. Climatol. **25**, 1965–1978 (2005). https://doi.org/10.1002/joc.1276
4. Pennington, T., Styles, B., Taylor, D.: Meliaceae. Monografía No. 28. Flora Neotropica, 395–400 (1981)
5. Mayhew, J., Newton, A.: The Silviculture of Mahogany. CAB International, London, England (1998)
6. Negreros-Castillo, P., Mize, C.: Soil-site preferences for mahogany (Swietenia macrophylla King) in the Yucatan Peninsula. New Forest. **44**(1), 85–99 (2013). https://doi.org/10.1007/s11056-011-9303-7
7. Snook, L.: Stand dynamics of mahogany (Swietenia macrophylla King) and associates species after fire and hurricane in the tropical forest of the Yucatan Peninsula, Mexico (Doctoral dissertation). Yale University, New Haven, CT, USA (1993)
8. Negreros-Castillo, P., et al.: Silviculture of the Mahogany Forest of Quintana Roo, Mexico: Criteria and Recommendations. CONAFOR, Mexico City, Mexico (2014)
9. Negreros-Castillo, P., Martínez-Salazar, I., Álvarez-Aquino, C., Navarro-Martínez, A., Mize, C.: Survival and growth of Swietenia macrophylla seedlings from seeds sown into slash and burn fields in Quintana Roo, Mexico. Bois et Forêts des Tropiques **337**, 17–26 (2018). https://doi.org/10.19182/bft2018.337.a31628
10. Figueroa, C.: An assessment of the distribution and status of Big-Leaf mahogany (Swietenia macrophylla King). In: Puerto Rico Conservation Foundation and International Institute of Tropical Forestry, Rio Piedras, Puerto Rico (1994)
11. Lamb, F.B.: Mahogany of Tropical America: Its Ecology and Management. University of Michigan, Ann Arbor, MI (1966)

12. Comisión Nacional Forestal: El Inventario Nacional Forestal y de Suelos México 2004–2009. Una herramienta que da certeza a la planeación, evaluación y el desarrollo forestal de México [The National Forest and Soil Inventory Mexico 2004–2009. A tool that gives certainty to the planning, evaluation, and forestry development of Mexico], Zapopan, México (2009)

13. Rodstrom, C., Olivieri, S., Tangley, L.: Un enfoque regional de la conservación en la Selva Maya [A regional approach to conservation in the Selva Maya]. In: Primack, R.B., Bray, D., Galletti, H.A., Ponciano, I. (eds.) La Selva Maya. Conservación y Desarrollo [The Mayan forest: Conservation and development], pp. 363–373. Siglo XXI Editores, Mexico City, Mexico (1999)

14. Ellis, E., Kainer, K.A., Sierra-Huelsz, J.A., Negreros-Castillo, P., DiGiano, M.: Community-based for management in Quintana Roo, Mexico. In: Cashore, B., de Jong, W.G., Galloway, P., Pacheco, P. (eds.) Forests Under Pressure: Local Responses to Global Issues, pp. 130–151. UFRO, Vienna, Austria (2014)

15. Weaver, P., Sabido, O.: Mahogany in Belize. International Institute of Tropical Forestry, US Department of Agriculture, Forest Service, Rio Piedras, Puerto Rico (1997)

16. Snook, L.: Sustaining harvests of mahogany from Mexico's Yucatan forests: past, present, and future, Chap. 5. In: Primack, R., Bray, D., Galletti, H., Ponciano, I. (eds.) Timber, Tourists and Temples: Conservation and Community Development in the Mayan Rainforest of Belize, Guatemala and Mexico, pp. 61–80. Island Press, Washington DC (1998)

17. Mejia, E., Buitrón, X., Pea-Claros, M., Grogan, J.: Big leaf mahogany (Swietenia macrophylla) in Peru, Bolivia and Brazil. In: NDF Workshop Case Studies, Cancún, Quintana Roo, México (2008)

18. Navarro-Martínez, M.A.: Diagnóstico del estado actual de Swietenia macrophylla King (caoba) en los bosques manejados de Quintana Roo, México: perspectivas para su manejo. Doctoral dissertation, México (2015)

19. Navarro, C., Wilson, J., Gillies, A., Hernández, M.: A new Mesoamerican collection of Big-Leaf Mahogany. In: Lugo, A.E., Figueroa Colón, J.C., Alayón, M. (eds.) Big-Leaf Mahogany. Ecological Studies (Analysis and Synthesis), vol. 159, pp. 103–114. Springer, New York (2003). https://doi.org/10.1007/0-387-21778-9_5

20. Newton, A.: Conservation of tree species through sustainable use: how can it be achieved in practice? Oryx **42**(2), 195–205 (2008). https://doi.org/10.1017/s003060530800759x

21. International Union for Conservation of Nature: The IUCN red list of threatened species (2010). http://www.iucnredlist.org. Accessed 4 Aug 2020

22. Grogan, J., Barreto, P.: Big-Leaf mahogany on CITES appendix II: big challenge, big opportunity. Conserv. Biol. **19**(3), 973–976 (2005)

23. Grogan, J., et al.: Over-harvesting driven by consumer demand leads to population decline: big-leaf mahogany in South America. Conserv. Lett. **3**(1), 12–20 (2010). https://doi.org/10.1111/j.1755-263x.2009.00082.x

24. Calvo, J., Rivera, H.: The state of mahogany in Mesoamerica. Report of the regional workshop. PROARCA/CAPAS, Costa Rica (2000)

25. Kommeter, R., Martinez, M., Blundell, A., Gullison, R., Steininger, M., Rice, R.: Impacts of unsustainable mahogany logging in Bolivia and Peru. Ecol. Soc. **9**(1), 12–23 (2004). https://doi.org/10.5751/es-00629-090112

26. Parmesan, C.: Ecological and evolutionary responses to recent climate change. Ann. Rev. Ecol. Evol. Syst. **37**, 637–669 (2006). https://doi.org/10.1146/annurev.ecolsys.37.091305.110100

27. Hof, C.: Species distributions and climate change: current patterns and future scenarios for biodiversity. Science University of Copenhagen, Department of Biology Faculty, Dinamarca (2010)
28. Anderson, R., Lew, D., Peterson, A.: Evaluating predictive models of species' distributions: criteria for selecting optimal models. Ecol. Model. **162**(3), 211–232 (2003). https://doi.org/10.1016/s0304-3800(02)00349-6
29. Saatchi, S., Buermann, W., ter Steege, H., Mori, S., Smith, T.: Modeling distribution of Amazonian tree species and diversity using remote sensing measurements. Remote Sens. Environ. **112**(5), 2000–2017 (2008). https://doi.org/10.1016/j.rse.2008.01.008
30. Mateo, R., Felicísimo, A., Muñoz, J.: Modelos de distribución de especies: Una revisión sintética. Revista chilena de historia natural **84**, 217–240 (2011). https://doi.org/10.4067/S0716-078X2011000200008
31. Martínez-Meyer, E., Díaz-Porras, D., Townsend, P., Yanez-Arenas, C.: Ecological niche structure and range wide abundance patterns of species. Biol. Lett. **9**, 1–5 (2013). https://doi.org/10.1098/rsbl.2012.0637
32. Merow, C., Smith, M., Silander, J.: A practical guide to MaxEnt for modeling species' distributions: what it does, and why inputs and settings matter. Ecography **36**(10), 1058–1069 (2013). https://doi.org/10.1111/j.1600-0587.2013.07872.x
33. Osorio-Olvera, L.A., Falconi, M., Soberón, J.: Sobre la relación entre idoneidad del hábitat y la abundancia poblacional bajo diferentes escenarios de dispersión. Revista Mexicana de Biodiversidad **87**, 1080–1088 (2016). https://doi.org/10.1016/j.rmb.2016.07.001
34. Phillips, S., Anderson, R., Schapire, R.: Maximum entropy modeling of species geographic distributions. Ecol. Model. **190**(3–4), 231–259 (2006). https://doi.org/10.1016/j.ecolmodel.2005.03.026
35. Phillips, S., Dudík, M.: Modeling of species distributions with MaxEnt: new extensions and a comprehensive evaluation. Ecography **31**(2), 161–175 (2008). https://doi.org/10.1111/j.0906-7590.2008.5203.x
36. Elith, J.H., et al.: Novel methods improve prediction of species' distributions from occurrence data. Ecography **29**(2), 129–151 (2006). https://doi.org/10.1111/j.2006.0906-7590.04596.x
37. Hernández-Gómez, I.U.: Evaluation of landscape transformation for the determination of priority conservation areas in the Uxpanapa region, Veracruz (Master's thesis). Universidad Veracruzana, Xalapa, Mexico, Tropical Research Center (2014)
38. Magaña, V., Conde, C., Sánchez, O., Gay, C.: Evaluación de escenarios regionales de clima actual y de cambio climático futuro para México. In: Gay, C. (ed.) En México: Una visión hacia el siglo XXI. El cambio climático en México, pp. 1–18. Instituto Nacional de Ecología, Universidad Nacional Autónoma de México, México (2003)
39. Gómez-Díaz, J.D., Monterroso-Rivas, A.I., Tinoco-Rueda, J.A.: Distribución del cedro rojo (Cedrela odorata L.) en el estado de Hidalgo, bajo condiciones actuales y escenarios de cambio climático. Madera y Bosques **13**(2), 29–49 (2007)
40. Villamonte-Cuneo, G.O.: Modelamiento del efecto del cambio climático en el nicho ecológico fundamental de especies de podocarpáceas peruanas en Sudamérica. Universidad Ricardo Palma, Tesis de Licenciatura en Biología (2018)
41. Soberón, J., Peterson, A.T.: Interpretation of models fundamental ecological niches and species distribution areas. Biodivers. Inform. **2**, 1–10 (2005)
42. Bellard, C., Bertelsmeier, C., Leadley, P., Thuiller, W., Courchamp, F.: Impacts of climate change on the future of biodiversity. Ecol. Lett. **15**(4), 365–377 (2012). https://doi.org/10.1111/j.1461-0248.2011.01736.x

43. Benito-Garzón, M., Sánchez-de Dios, R., Sainz-Ollero, H.: Effects of climate change on the distribution of Iberian tree species. Appl. Veg. Sci. **11**(2), 169–178 (2008). https://doi.org/10.3170/2008-7-18348

44. Leguía, E.J., Locatelli, B., Imbach, P.: Impacto del cambio climático en plantaciones forestales en Centroamérica. Recursos Naturales y Ambiente **56–57**, 150–159 (2009). http://repositorio.bibliotecaorton.catie.ac.cr

45. Benito-Garzón, M., Alía, R., Robson, T.M., Zavala, M.A.: Intra-specific variability and plasticity influence potential tree species distributions under climate change. Glob. Ecol. Biogeogr. **20**, 766–778 (2011). https://doi.org/10.1111/j.1466-8238.2010.00646.x

46. Benito-Garzón, M., Ruiz-Benito, P., Zavala, M.A.: Interspecific inferences in tree growth and mortality responses to environmental drivers determine potential species distributional limits in Iberian forests. Glob. Ecol. Biogeogr. **22**, 1141–1151 (2013). https://doi.org/10.1111/geb.12075

47. Gutiérrez, E., Trejo, I.: Efecto del cambio climático en la distribución potencial de cinco especies arbóreas de bosque templado en México. Revista Mexicana de Biodiversidad **85**, 179–188 (2014). https://doi.org/10.7550/rmb.37737

48. Garza-López, M., Ortega-Rodríguez, J., Zamudio-Sánchez, F., López-Toledo, J., Domínguez-Álvarez, F., Sáenz-Romero, C.: Calakmul como refugio de Swietenia macrophylla King ante el cambio climático [Calakmul as a refuge for Swietenia macrophylla King in the face of climate change]. Bot. Sci. **94**(1), 43 (2016). https://doi.org/10.17129/botsci.500

49. Guisan, A., Zimmermann, N., Elith, J., Graham, C., Phillips, S., Peterson, A.: What matters for predicting the occurrences of trees: techniques, data, or species' characteristics? Ecol. Monogr. **77**(4), 615–630 (2007). https://doi.org/10.1890/06-1060.1

50. Ramírez-Magil, G., Botello-López, F., Navarro Martínez, A.: Idoneidad de hábitat para Swietenia macrophylla en escenarios de cambio climático en México. Madera y Bosques (in press)

51. Espinosa-Organista, D., Ocegueda-Cruz, S., Aguilar-Zúñiga, C., Flores-Villela, O., Llorente-Bousquets, J.: El conocimiento biogeográfico de las especies y su regionalización natural. En Capital natural de México, pp. 33–65. CONABIO, México (2008)

52. Osorio-Olvera, L., Barve, V., Barve, N., Soberón, J., Falconi, M.: Ntbox: From getting biodiversity data to evaluating species distribution models in a friendly GUI environment. R package version 0.2.5.4 (2018). https://github.com/luismurao/ntbox

Index of Coastal Urban Resilience (ICURHF) When Coping with Hurricanes and Floods in the City of Chetumal, in the South East of Mexico

José Manuel Camacho-Sanabria[1]([✉]) [iD], Rosalía Chávez-Alvarado[1]([✉]) [iD], Juan Antonio Álvarez-Trinidad[2] [iD], and David Velázquez-Torres[2] [iD]

[1] Chetumal Academic Unit, Conacyt, Quintana Roo University, Mexico, Mexico
jmanuelcs@live.com.mx, rosaliadf@gmail.com
[2] Chetumal Academic Unit, Quintana Roo University, Mexico, Mexico
jaatalvarez@gmail.com, davvelaz@gmail.com

Abstract. The topic of resilience is essential in the natural disaster risk public management, which influences the quality of life of the people nowadays, specifically in the coastal cities that are the ones that in a near future will be more affected by hurricanes, and atypical rainfall, derived from the climatic change. There are various initiatives or agreements that contributed with evidence to commence the works focused on the increase of resilience in the cities, the most recent one is the Framework of Sendai 2015–2030, which promoted from public policies to global ones, such as the guide to determine resilience. This work proposes the introduction of an Index of Coastal Urban Resilience when coping with Hurricanes and Floods (ICURHF) of an urban location situated in the south east of Mexico (Chetumal). The Index is integrated by three components: Menace, Vulnerability and Capacity of Adaptation, each of them has a determined number of simple indicators which were classified, standardized, and assessed based on the technique known as judgment of experts. The results show that 60% of the city has a high resilience on the account of the indicators originated from the knowledge of the population about the risk of disasters - they are exposed to – when coping with the impact of hurricanes and floods. The remaining 40% registers a medium resilience corresponding to the Basic Geostatistical Areas (BGA's) where the Menace is very high, and the Vulnerability is high. The principal contribution of this Index is the inclusion of qualitative indicators which strengthen the definition of resilience as a social construct.

Keywords: Flood · Hurricane · Resilience · Vulnerability

We would like to thank Gerardo Quiroz Almaraz for his support in the translation.
Project financiad by Conacyt 248375, called: Resiliencia en ciudades costeras del Caribe Mexicano ante desastres por huracanes: Chetumal, Tulum y Playa del Carmen.

M. F. Mata-Rivera et al. (Eds.): GIS LATAM 2020, CCIS 1276, pp. 136–150, 2020.
https://doi.org/10.1007/978-3-030-59872-3_10

1 Introduction

One of the objectives in the world agenda is to deal with the resilience when coping with Hydrometeorological phenomena, based on the reports of the Intergovernmental Panel of Climatic Change (IPCC) which indicate that the menaces of natural origin will occur with higher intensity and magnitude.

Resilience as a connected concept to the risk of disaster is framed in the definitions of social vulnerability, adaptation capacity, and menace. Vulnerability was defined as a direct relation with resilience, some time ago. According to Holling, in 1973, and Gallopin, in 2006, there is a change in time in the relation between the human being and the nature, from the vision of the socioecological systems, where domains of attraction exist, that is to say what is usually known as indicators which explain the results and consequences of such relation human being and the nature [1, 2].

One of the most relevant events related with the risk of disasters was the flood of the Mississippi river in 1927, which provoked the evacuations of 600 000 people, approximately [3]. The first international conference against national calamities was held in Paris in 1937, and the theory of extreme values by Gumbel for the estimate of areas and degrees of the risk of flood was formulated in 1941 [4].

The first studies that included the perception, and the human behavior in the analysis of risks were developed in the 1970s, the fundaments of a theory of catastrophe were, as well, established, then [5, 6]. The works of the 1980s were focused on the correlation between natural danger, and underdevelopment, the improvement of the studies of man-generated risks, and the multidisciplinary recognition, which is required for the study of the risks [7].

The Latin-American Council of Social Sciences (LACSC) allowed its position to be glimpsed when it came to the relation between the condition of the population and the present difficulties in a situation of risk in 1985 [8]. The International Decade for the reduction of natural disasters was declared in the 1990s; its principal objective was to diminish disasters through a higher surveillance, and knowledge of the natural menaces from the scientific and technical point of view [9]. This initiative contributed to the establishment of the Network of social studies for the prevention of natural disasters in Latin America (La RED).

The measures that the scientific community, national governments, and regional organisms, and international organizations elaborated at the beginning of the decade, to prevent and mitigate the disasters, were examined by regional, national, and international groups from 155 countries and territories during the World Conference on the Reduction of National Disasters in the middle of the decade. This analysis, as well as the orientations for the future were recapitulated in the Message, Strategy, and Plan of Action of Yokohama for a Safer World [10]. The latter was the reference so that more concrete actions related to the diminishment of risk could be promoted as well as stated during the Framework of action of Yogo 2005–2015 [11]. The world campaign "Developing Resilient Cities; My City is getting Ready", whose objective was to promote and boost the commitment of local governments so that the diminishment of risk and the resilience of disasters could be a priority of their policies, was instrumented by the office of the United Nations for the reduction of disaster risk (UNISDR) in 2010, taking advantage of the Framework of Action of Hyogo in order to address more closely the local necessities [12].

The Framework of Sendai for the Reduction of disaster risk 2015–2030, successor instrument of the Framework of Action of Hyogo – which continues recognizing the objective of reducing every type of loss provoked by disasters – was approved in 2015; conducting the international efforts related to the topic until 2030 as well as sharing strategies of action with the purpose of achieving better results than in the first ten years [13]. This initiative has demonstrated that some countries take advantage of the information and allow databases which permit the planning of prevention, mitigation, response, recovery, and reconstruction.

Other initiatives, orientated to raise awareness and get the cities ready for the construction of resilience when coping with social, economic and physical challenges that they will have to face in an even more urbanized world, have been developed in recent years. Out of those initiatives, the challenge 100 Resilient cities of Rockefeller Foundation, Resilient Cities Profile Program (CRPP) of the United Nations, Habitat, and New Urban Agenda stand out among them [14, 15].

Actions to deal with the international commitments related to the diminishment of the environmental risks in urban areas were commenced by Mexico after the latter initiatives were developed.

Some of the principal actions were consultation, revision, and modification of some of the national laws related to the environment, territorial ordering and risks which were disassociated from international agreements as well as from the reality of the country. In some cases, the decree of new laws was indispensable.

In 2012, the General Law of Climatic Change, which foresees two indispensable instruments to orient and instrument the public policy in the subject: The National Strategy of Climatic Change and the Special Program of Climatic Change 2013–2018 [16], was published. The General Law of Human Settlements, currently known as General Law of Human Settlements, Territorial Ordering, and Urban Development) that strengthens the bases of the public management in human settlements, was modified.

Together with the latter, there are recent domestic initiatives and works that have been developed with the objective of diminishing the vulnerability and increase the resilience when coping with the impact of diverse menaces such as the Network of Resilient Cities for Mexico and the Guide of Resilience which was developed with the goal of strengthening and orienting local governments to prevent, cope with, and respond to disasters immediately. Nowadays, there are profiles of resilience principally in the following cities of these Mexican states: Playa del Carmen and Cozumel (Quintana Roo), La Paz (Baja California Sur), Tijuana (Baja California Norte), Ciudad Juárez (Chihuahua) Manzanillo (Colima), Allende (Nuevo León).

On the other hand, it must be considered that Mexico is one of the most vulnerable countries to the effects of climatic change, especially due to its location set in a continuously exposed region – which is frequently hit by the impact of hurricanes and affected by floods. Chetumal is a coastal city located in the south east of Mexico, and ever since it was founded (previously known as Payo Obispo back in 1904) until nowadays different hydro-meteorogical phenomena of this kind have been registered, which have caused

Table 1. Hurricanes that have caused damages to the city of Chetumal

Name/Date	Damages
Hurricane/1910	650 people were affected by this natural menace amidst the absence of basic services
Hurricane/10–1916	It destroyed houses, provoked floods, and caused collateral damage (Death toll: 84 malaria victims)
Hurricane/09–1931	No record of damages known
Hurricane/08–1934	It generated floods, as a result of a cyclonic disturbance that affected Belize and the coasts of Campeche
Santa Mónica/08–1942	It generated a few damages in dwellings and public spaces facilities as well as the decrease of lands of crop
Hurricane/11–1942	It destroyed parks, docks, public buildings, and houses, impacted the forest activity apart from causing insalubrity problems
Janet/09 –1955	Death toll: 84 people as well as a large number of missing people, 80% of the infrastructure was destroyed, and the cover of the jungle was lost
Carmen/09–1974	It generated floods particularly near the harbor area and damages to the public infrastructure and dwellings; electricity and water supplies were interrupted, and the surrounding jungle was gravely affected
Gert/09–1993	It generated enormous puddles and floods in the lower area of the city (evacuation of the inhabitants)
Opal y Roxanne/09 y 10–1995	Payo Obispo, the water supply was also suspended in 60% of the city
Mitch/10–1998	There were floods that affected approximately 70 families in Fidel Velázquez and Proterritorio neighborhoods (The flood level reached 50 cm); Nueva Reforma and 5 de Abril neighborhoods were also affected by the floods
Dean/08–2007	It affected nine hundred thousand hectares of forest vegetation and generated severe floods in low-leveled areas of the city
Karl/09–2010	157 mm of rainfall were recorded in approximately three hours, generating floods in 40 neighborhoods

(continued)

Table 1. (*continued*)

Name/Date	Damages
Ernesto and Tropical Wave No.11/08–2012	They caused several enormous puddles and floods (210 mm of rainfall were recorded in 12 h)
Tropical Wave No. 11/08–2015.	There were floods in several neighborhoods, roads, contiguous zones to the harbor (200 mm of rainfall were recorded in 12 h)
Earl /08–2016	Floods in critical areas in the city
Tropical Wave No. 3/06–2018	There were floods in Comité Proterritorio neighborhood, the emergency program "Operativo Tormenta" was activated with the purpose of helping the affected population
Tropical Wave No. 29/06–2019	It generated floods in the Proterritorio neighborhood, automobiles were stuck in the flooded streets
Tropical storm Amada Tropical storm Cristóbal/06–2020	Accumulated water exceeded 50 cm of height. In some neighborhoods, the Monument of the Fisher, located near the bay, was also affected by the flood because of the storm tide effect

Source: Chart elaborated by the authors based upon [17–23].

floods turning in human, economic, infrastructural, and environmental damages (see Table 1).

In the presence of this panorama, the present work suggests a proposal of Index of Coastal Urban Resilience (ICURHF) which allows the integration of indicators to evaluate the conditions of menace, vulnerability and capacity of adaptation of the city of Chetumal located in the south east of Mexico.

2   Methodology

2.1   Area of Study

Chetumal, capital city of the Mexican state of Quintana Roo, is a coastal city of the Mexican Caribbean; it is located between the parallels 18°, 33′, 46″ and 18°, 29′, 40″ north latitude, and between the meridians 88°, 21′, 57″ and 88°, 16′, 45″ west longitude. It is adjacent with the Bay of Chetumal, to the east, and the Río Hondo – the natural limit in the borderline with Belize – to the south, the wetlands La Sabana, to the west, and the lagoon system of Bacalar (see Fig. 1).

The criteria of selection of the area of study were established based upon two principal aspects: a) The exponential demographic growth reported by INEGI (Informatic, Geography and Statistical National Institute, in English) during the decade between 2000–2010 (2.2%), which was higher than the annual national growth rate (1.4%) [26], and b) the continuous hurricane menace, as well as the exposure to it; tropical waves or storms that are originated in the Atlantic Ocean and the Pacific Ocean.

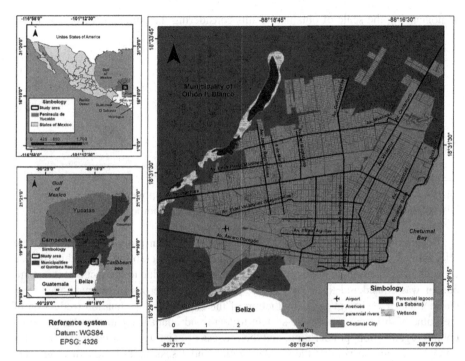

Fig. 1. Geographical location of the area of study in the national, regional, state, and municipality context [24, 25].

2.2 Methods and Materials

In order to demarcate the index of coastal urban resilience (ICURHF), a conceptual model and a system of indicators of coastal urban resilience were previously elaborated, both instruments were sustained in the framework of reference that encompasses (national and international) initiatives, agreements, strategies, actions, and methodologies associated with the prevention and mitigation of disasters, disaster risk public management, and urban resilience. The construction of the conceptual model and the system of indicators was developed based upon participative workshops (between professor-researchers and postgraduate students), semi-structured interviews with key actors and a survey which was applied in 450 private inhabited dwellings [27, 28].

The conceptual model and the system of indicators was structured in three components: menace, vulnerability, and capacity of adaptation. The system of indicators was integrated by a simple indicator ensemble which were selected by the following criteria: a) availability of sources (access to sources of data) b) pertinence (To contribute to decision taking), c) comprehension (to promote credibility and reliability of the users), d) comparability (local, municipal, state, regional, and national analysis) e) prediction capacity (to warn problems, risks and significant changes).

A total of 28 simple indicators were established, which were classified as positive (contributing to the resilience, and negative ones influencing the stability and/or the decrease of the resilience). A standardization by rank was applied with the purpose of homogenizing the scale of obtained results considering the parameters from 0 to 1 as well as the following formulas [29, 30]:

$$Positive = \frac{x - VMin}{VMax - VMin} \tag{1}$$

$$Negative = \frac{VMax - x}{VMax - VMin} \tag{2}$$

Where:

X = Brute value of the simple indicator j in the component i.
$VMin$ = Minimal value of the simple indicator j in the component i.
$VMax$ = Maximum value of the simple indicator j in the component i.

Regarding the ponderation (P_i) of the indicators, equi-proportional values were selected and utilized for the components menace and vulnerability (2.5) while for the capacity of adaptation an ponderation of 0.5 was assigned due to the fact that this component was considered to be part of one of the key properties of the resilience from the moment it assists in construction of the capacity of attenuation (reduction of the vulnerability) permitting the system to learn and adapt itself to the change based upon reorganization, ponderation, and the process of existing knowledge [31, 32]. It is important to emphasize that the standardization and assessment of the indicators were established based on the technique judgment of experts (see Tables 2, 3, and 4).

Table 2. Simple indicators for menace components of ICURHF

Context	Indicator	Ponderation
Natural	% of rainfall flooding area	−0.4
	% of storm tide flooding area	−0.6
		$\sum -1.0$

Source: Table elaborated by the authors based upon [25].

The calculation of ICURHF and its components, it was necessary to use the ponderation, that is to say, numeric ponderation or percentages which were associated according to the relevance of the component [29, 34–36]. The Index of coastal urban resilience was determined based upon the following formula:

$$ICURHF = C_1 * P_1 + C_2 * P_2 + C_3 * P_3; \forall P_i \neq 0 \tag{3}$$

Where:

$ICURHF$ = Index of coastal urban resilience
C_i = Component i in the Index of coastal urban resilience

Table 3. Simple indicators for vulnerability components of ICURHF

Context	Indicator	Ponderation
Natural	Population Density	−0.09
	% of infantile population (0–14)	−0.07
	% of 65-year-old or older population	−0.07
Social	% of non-rightful claimant to healthcare service population	−0.07
	% of handicapped population	−0.07
	% of 15-year-old, or older, and illiterate population	−0.07
Economic	% of non-economically active	−0.07
	Population % of censual homes with female leadership	−0.07
	% of inhabited private dwellings with earth floor	−0.07
	% of inhabited private one-room dwellings	−0.07
Constructed	% of inhabited private dwellings without services	−0.07
	% of inhabited private dwellings	−0.07
	% threatened by flood risk	−0.07
Cultural	% of the population who ignores their location is hurricane-prone	−0.07
	% of the population who has not experienced a hurricane yet	−0.07
		$\sum -1.0$

Source: Table elaborated by the authors based upon [25, 27, 28, 33].

$P_i=$ Ponderation of the component in the calculation of the Index of coastal urban resilience

$$\sum\nolimits_{i=1}^{3} P_i = P_1 + P_2 + P_3 = 1 \tag{4}$$

Where:

In the same way, the result of every component is obtained through the ponderation mean of the simple indicators considered in each one of them.

$$C_i = \sum\nolimits_{i=1}^{ni} I_{i,j} * P_{i,j} = I_{I,1} * P_{I,1} + I_{I,2} * P_{I,2} + \ldots + I_{i,ni} * P_{i,ni}; \forall P_{i,j} \neq 0 \tag{5}$$

Where:

$I_{i,j} =$ Simple indicator j which is used for the calculation of ICURHF in the component i.

$P_{i,j} =$ Assigned ponderation to the simple indicator j in the calculation of ICURHF in the component i.

Table 4. Simple indicators for capacity of adaptation components of ICURHF

Context	Indicator	Ponderation
Social	% of the population who has dwelled in the city for over 5 years	0.03
Economic	% of inhabited private dwellings where 2, or more, [family members] work	0.03
Natural	% of green areas	0.02
Constructed	% of inhabited private dwellings with insurance	0.04
Cultural	% of inhabited private dwellings which count on an emergency plan	0.2
	Risk atlas	0.15
	Plan of urban development	0.1
	% of inhabited private dwellings where, at least, a family member has been trained to know what to do in case a hurricane hits or in the event of floods	0.2
	% of inhabited private dwellings where, at least, a family member has received information about what to do in the event of a hurricane, or flood	0.04
Institutional	% of the population who knows government, and non-government programs that promote the prevention of risks in the event of a hurricane or a flood	0.04
	% of the population who knows the location of the closest temporary shelter	0.1
	% of the population who knows the routes of evacuation in the event of a flood or a hurricane	0.05
		$\sum 1.0$

Source: Table elaborated by the authors based upon [25, 27, 28, 33].

$$\sum\nolimits_{j=1}^{ni} P_{i,j} = P_{i,1} + P_{i,2} + \ldots + P_{i,ni} = 1 \tag{6}$$

With the goal of spatially representing on a BGA (Basic Geostatistical Area) scale, the obtained results from every component and, consequently, from ICURHF, the following ordinal scale was established (See Table 5).

Table 5. Nominal scale to spatially represent ICURHF

Interval	Scale
0%–39.9%	Low
40%–59.9%	Medium
60%–79.9%	High
80%–100%	Very High

Source: Adapted by the authors based upon [29, 34, 35].

3   Results and Discussion

In the Fig. 2a, the spatial distribution of the indicators of the menace component can be observed, the very high values correspond to the BGA's with a surface flooded by storm tide higher or equal to 80% (Del Bosque, 5 de Abril, Nueva Reforma, Plutarco Elías Calles, Centro and Aarón Medino neighborhoods are principally located in these areas), the BGA's with high values in zones that are flooded by a 60 to 79.9% of rainfall or storm tide (Proterritorio, Primera Legislatura, Andrés Quintana Roo, Solidaridad, Nuevo Progreso, Fidel Velázquez, and Adolfo López Mateos neighborhoods are located there). Both menaces (coastal flood and pluvial flood) cause damages in the dwellings, as well as in the road infrastructure and, at the same time, deteriorate the quality of life of its inhabitants. The Comission of Drinking Water and Sewerage of Chetumal has located 124 locations that have problems of flood and enormous puddles in the city [17].

Regarding the vulnerability, Fig. 2b shows that 67% of the GBA's that compound the city, registered high vulnerability while 22% correspond to medium vulnerability, 7% to the low one, 2% to the high one, and 2% is non-applicable (regarding the airport and residential areas which are not included in this study due to lack of access to the information). The areas with very high and high vulnerability are associated to: 1) dwellings at risk of floods (48%), principally the ones located in the nearby area of the harbor and the wetlands called La Sabana, as well as the neighborhoods previously listed, and 2) the population that has never experienced a hurricane hitting (54%). Regarding this [20], states the affectations that have caused the different hurricanes in the city of Chetumal, from its foundation until hurricane Earl hit in 2016. He mentions that most [of the damages] are floods in the nearby area of the bay, as well as in some neighborhoods referred in the previous paragraph.

Additionally, 58% of the BGA's reported high capacity of adaptation, 33% very high, 4% low, 3% medium, and 2% non-applicable (see Fig. 2c). The high values of this component are principally related with the updated Plan of Urban Development (100% corresponds to the year 2018) the dwelling where inhabitants have received information about what to do in case of the event of a hurricane or a flood (93%), the population that knows the location of the nearest temporary anticyclonic shelter (68%), and the population who is familiar with programs that promote prevention of risks as a result of a hurricane or a flood (56%).

According to Rodriguez [20], during the last decades there has been an intense media bombing in Chetumal regarding what to do before, during, and after the event of a hurricane. Notwithstanding the difficulties, state authorities have been exclusively concerned in the preparation and recovery of the population, emphasizing that the institutional decisions are still centered in an emergency nevertheless, they are not actions centered in the processes of mitigation of risks.

The presence of indicators, whose values are low, and have an effect on the capacity of adaptation is also emphasized, for instance: The Atlas of Risks to scale of the city (50%), it is not updated, solely the 1.8% of the surveyed dwellings have a Plan of Familial Emergency, 7% of the dwellings have insurance, 29% of the inhabitants of the dwellings have been trained in relation to what to do in the event of a hurricane, or a flood, and 31% of the population knows the routes of evacuation when coping with a hurricane or a flood. Vis-à-vis the Atlas of Risks, this planning instrument was elaborated for the city of Chetumal in 2005, and it was the first approximation to the study of risk in this territory and locations within the Plan of Urban Development of the Suburban Area. This instrument was updated in 2011 with the purpose of identifying, in addition to locating, the type and grade of risk for geological and hydrometeorological phenomena, as well as their vulnerability [25]. In the last years, in the presence of the demographic growth of this city, together with the effects of the climatic change, it is compelling to bring the Atlas of Risks of Chetumal up to date based on methodologies that take into consideration the urban hydrographic analysis with the purpose of obtaining the identification and zoning of the areas at risk of floods [37].

The ICURHF of the city of Chetumal, on a BGA scale, showed that 60% of it has a high resilience, in the meantime the rest of the area (40%) registered a medium resilience. The latter corresponds to the BGA's where the menace was very high, and the vulnerability high. The ICURHF of Chetumal, at a city level, was of 63% (see Fig. 2d). This datum is approximated to the Index of hurricane risk in Chetumal (69%) corresponding to the impact of hurricane Dean in 2007 [38]. At the other end of the spectrum, Martínez et al., in 2018, got the Index of resilience in the infrastructure of drinking water of the city of Chetumal when coping with hurricanes: which was of 69% [39]. Frausto et al., in 2018, reported a medium level of resilience for the island of Cozumel (situated in the south east of Mexico) that was determined based on the integration of simple indicators and derived composed by the conduction of a representative survey. Participative methods, for the assignation of the ponderations, were utilized, as well [40].

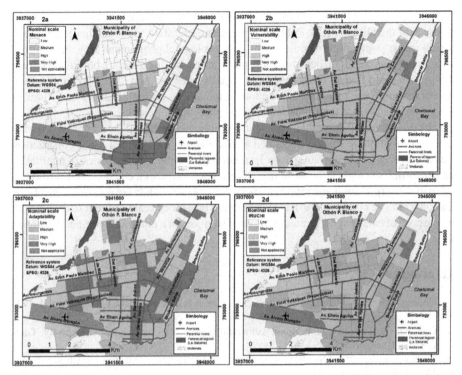

Fig. 2. Index of menace, vulnerability and capacity of adaptation and resilience Chetumal [24, 25, 27, 28, 33].

4 Conclusion

The studies of resilience when coping with disaster risks are still scarce. Furthermore, it is observed that the concept of resilience in diverse work as an adjective for communities, and people, which is correct in the face of the study of phenomena that involve the population, Nevertheless, in the Guide of Resilient Cities it can be observed that these are tangible elements, and not people, which are evaluated for the resilience; that is the reason why in this work an exercise is done which considers the inhabitants of the city of Chetumal, and their knowledge regarding the risk of hurricanes and floods that they have acquired through life experience, as well as via different mass media. This aspect was decisive in the process of assignation of weights of each one of the components that integrated the index, since the indicators of Menace and Vulnerability depend on the (physical, natural, and social) characteristics of the city – to a greater extent- and not on the knowledge of the population about the risk, that is the reason why a higher ponderation of the indicators of the component Capacity of Adaptation was assigned.

The Index of Coastal Urban Resilience when coping with hurricanes and floods (ICURHF) of Chetumal combines a series of simple indicators associated to the natural, social, economic, cultural, institutional, as well as the dwelling, conditions that characterize this coastal city.

Even though the ICURHF turned out to be high, it is compelling to train, from the approach of the Disaster Risk Public Management, (the state and municipal) authorities as well as the population regarding hydrometeorological phenomena they are continuously living together with, because both parts reaffirm having a culture before the impact of hurricanes and floods, when they have actually been focused on the preparation and recovery when these menaces hit, without emphasizing on the measures or actions of mitigation of risks that contribute to the prevention of future risks.

The proposed Index, in this work, can be replicated, adapted, and improved for the development of future studies associated with resilience in the light of risks of disasters in coastal cities, or in other urban spaces. Its main contribution is the inclusion of qualitative indicators that strengthen the definition of resilience as a social construct. Nevertheless, the spatial interpretation and representation of the obtained data are presented on a BGA scale; it would be convenient to have information on a block scale, in order to design with the purpose of establishing strategies of local solution on a community or neighborhood scale.

References

1. Holling, C.S.: Resilience and stability of ecological systems. Ann. Rev. Ecol. Syst. **4**, 1–23 (1973)
2. Gallopín, G.C.: Linkages between vulnerability, resilience, and adaptive capacity. Glob. Environ. Change **16**(3), 293–303 (2006)
3. Congress of the United States: Ley de control de Inundaciones 70°, Sess, 1. Ch.596, 5 May 1928, Unites States (1928)
4. Vilches, O.R., Reyes, C.M.: Riesgos naturales: evolución y modelos conceptuales. Review Universitaria de Geografía **20**(1), 83–116 (2011)
5. García-Tornel, F.C.: La Geografía de los Riesgos. Review Geocrítica, Cuadernos Críticos de geografía humana **54**, 5–40 (1984)
6. Ayala-Carcedo, F.J., Olcina-Cantos, J.: Riesgos naturales. Editorial Ariel, Barcelona, Spain (2002)
7. de Castro, S.D.A., Riesgos y Peligros: Una visión desde la geografía. Scripta Nova. Electronic Review of Geografía y Ciencias Sociales **4**(60), 55–78 (2000)
8. Lovón-Zavala, G., Caputo, M.G., Hardoy, J.E., Herzer, H.M.: Desastres naturales y sociedad en América Latina. Buenos Aires. Argentina. Grupo Editor Latinoamericano (1985)
9. Lavell, A.: Comunidades urbanas, vulnerabilidad desastres y opciones de prevención y mitigación: Una propuesta de investigación-acción para Centroamérica en: Viviendo en Riesgo. Chapter 2. LA RED: https://www.desenredando.org/public/libros/1994/ver/html/3cap2.htm (1997). Accessed 01 Aug 2020
10. United Nations - EIRD. Conferencia Mundial sobre desastres. Yokohama: ONU. https://eird.org/fulltext/Yokohama-strategy/YokohamaEspa%F1ol.pdf (1994). Accessed 01 Aug 2020
11. United Nations. Hyogo Framework for Action 2005–2015: Building the Resilience of Nations and Communities to Disasters. International Strategy for Disaster Reduction. World Conference on Disaster Reduction 18–22 January 2005, Kobe, Hyogo, Japan. https://www.unisdr.org/2005/wcdr/intergover/official-doc/L-docs/Hyogo-framework-for-action-english.pdf. Accessed 01 Aug 2020
12. United Nations. Cómo desarrollar ciudades más resilientes. Un manual para los líderes de los gobiernos locales. Una contribución a la Campaña Mundial 2010–2015 "Desarrollando ciudades resilientes - ¡Mi ciudad se está preparando!". March 2012, Ginebra. https://www.unisdr.org/files/26462_manualparalideresdelosgobiernosloca.pdf. Accessed 01 Aug 2020

13. ONU. Marco de Sendai para la Reducción del Riesgo de Desastres 2015–2030. https://www.unisdr.org/files/43291_spanishsendaiframeworkfordisasterri.pdf (2015). Accessed 01 Apr 2020
14. Galcerán, M.L.: reducción del riesgo de los desastres Translación de la agenda global de resiliencia al ámbito local. Notas internacionales CIDOB **117**, 1–5 (2015)
15. United Nations. Nueva Agenda Urbana H III. A Conferencia de las Naciones Unidas sobre la Vivienda y el Desarrollo Urbano Sostenible (Hábitat III). Quito, Ecuador, el 20 de octubre de 2016. http://habitat3.org/wp-content/uploads/NUA-Spanish.pdf. Accessed 30 May 2020
16. Natural Resources and Environmental Secretary. Versión de difusión del Programa Especial de Cambio Climático 2014–2018. México: Secretaría de Medio Ambiente y Recursos Naturales. http://www.sectur.gob.mx/wp-content/uploads/2014/09/PECC-2014-2018.pdf (2014). Accessed 27 Jan 2020
17. CAPA-IMTA. Informe del Programa para el Manejo del Agua Pluvial de la Ciudad de Chetumal, Quintana Roo. Comisión de Agua Potable y Alcantarillado (CAPA) and Instituto Mexicano de Tecnología del Agua (IMTA). Cuernavaca, México (2013)
18. Morales, J.J.: Selvas, mares y huracanes. Gobierno del estado de Yucatán y Biblioteca básica de Yucatán. Mérida, México (2012)
19. Morales, J.J.: Quintana Roo, Tierra de Huracanes. En Carlos Macías Richard (Coord.). Quintana Roo: Vitalidad histórica y despliegue contemporáneo. Tomo II, pp. 144–161. Agencia Promotora de Publicaciones, México (2016)
20. Alarcón, M.N.R.: Convivir con la amenaza, vulnerabilidad y riesgo frente a los huracanes en la ciudad de Chetumal, Quintana Roo. Thesis for Master in Social Antropology. Universidad de Quintana Roo, México (2017)
21. Secretaría de Desarrollo Agrario, Territorial y Urbano SEDATU. Programa de Desarrollo Urbano de Chetumal, Calderitas, Subteniente López, Huay-Pix y Xul-há. Municipio de Othón P. Blanco. http://www.opb.gob.mx/portal/wp-content/uploads/transparencia/93/I/f/PDU2018/PDU%20integrado%2019012018-publicacion%20digital.pdf (2018). Accessed 01 Aug 2020
22. Maiza, X., Ángel, J.: Enciclopedia de Quintana Roo. Fascículo Historia, Quintana Roo, México (2004)
23. Maiza, X., Ángel, J.: Enciclopedia de Quintana Roo. Fascículo Chetumal, Quintana Roo México (2005)
24. Instituto Nacional de Estadística y Geografía INEGI. Marco Geoestadístico, Datos Vectoriales, México (2016)
25. Centro de Información Geográfica-Universidad de Quintana Roo CIG-UQROO. Atlas de Riesgo de la ciudad de Chetumal, Municipio de Othón P. Blanco, Quintana Roo. México. http://rmgir.proyectomesoamerica.org/PDFMunicipales/2011/vr_23004_AR_OTHON_P_BLANCO.pdf (2011). Accessed 01 Aug 2020
26. Instituto Nacional de Estadística y Geografía INEGI. *Censo de Población y Vivienda 2010. Perfil sociodemográfico: Estados Unidos Mexicanos*. México. http://internet.contenidos.inegi.org.mx/contenidos/Productos/prod_serv/contenidos/espanol/bvinegi/productos/censos/poblacion/2010/perfil_socio/uem/702825047610_1.pdf (2013). Accessed 27 July 2020
27. Sanabria, J.M.C., Alvarado, R.C., Torres, D.V.:. Propuesta Metodológica para Medir la Resiliencia Urbana ante Huracanes e Inundaciones en el Caribe Mexicano. Rev. REDER **3**(2), 28–43 (2019)
28. Alvarado, R.C., Sanabria, J.M.C., Torres, D.V.: El camino hacia un modelo metodológico para realizar un índice de resiliencia en ciudades costeras (IRCC) del Caribe mexicano ante huracanes e inundaciones. Review Contexto **XIII**(18), 13–29 (2019)
29. Villanueva, L.C., et al.: Modelo de indicadores para la evaluación y monitoreo del desarrollo sustentable en la zona costera de Mahahual. Quintana Roo, México. Perspectiva Geográfica **19**(2), 309–330 (2014)

30. Miranda, J.P.R., Suazo, Á., Malfanti, I.S.: Análisis por medio de la normalización de variables para un modelo de planificación ambiental hídrica estacional. Obras y proyectos **20**, 76–85 (2016). http://dx.doi.org/10.4067/S0718-28132016000200006

31. Jacobi, J., Schneider, M., Pillco Mariscal, M.I., Huber, S., Weidmann, S., Rist, S.: La contribución de la producción del cacao orgánico a la resiliencia socio-ecológica en el contexto del cambio climático en el Alto Beni - La Paz. Acta Nova **6**(4), 351–383 (2014)

32. Jeans, H., Castillo, G.E. Thomas, S.: L'avenir est un choix. Absorption, adaptation et transformation: Les capacités de résilience. Oxfam International. https://oxfamilibrary.ope nrepository.com/bitstream/handle/10546/620178/gd-resilience-capacities-absorbadapt-tra nsform-250117-fr.pdf?sequence=6&isAllowed=y (2017). Accessed 04 Aug 2019

33. Instituto Nacional de Estadística y Geografía INEGI. Censo de Población y Vivienda 2010. Principales resultados por AGEB y manzana urbana. México (2010)

34. Leva, G.: Indicadores de calidad de vida urbana. Teoría y metodología. Universidad Nacional de Quilmes, Argentina (2005)

35. Villanueva, L.C.: Urbanización, problemas ambientales y calidad de vida urbana. Plaza y Valdés, Ciudad de México, México (2009)

36. Nieves, A., Domínguez, F.C.: Probabilidad y estadística para ingeniería: Un enfoque moderno, 1a edn. McGraw-Hill, México (2010)

37. Chaparro, M., Carlos, J.: Mapping the Risk of Flood, Mass Movement and Local Subsidence. Springer, Switzerland (2020)

38. Hernández, M.L., Carreño, M.L., Castillo, L.: Methodologies and tolos of risk management: Hurricane risk index (HRi). Int. J. Disaster Risk Reduct. **31**, 926–937 (2018). https://doi.org/10.1016/j.ijdrr.2018.08.006

39. Méndez, A.M., Martínez, O.F., Villanueva, L.C., Sanabria, J.M.C.: Índice de Resiliencia de Infraestructura de agua potable ante huracanes en ciudades costeras **61E**(3), 339–365 (2018). http://dx.doi.org/10.15359/rgac.Esp-3.17

40. Martínez, O.F., et al.: Perfil de resiliencia urbana de la isla de Cozumel, México. Antrópica, Revista de Ciencias Sociales y Humanidades **4**(8), 215–237 (2018). https://antropica.com. mx/ojs2/index.php/AntropicaRCSH/article/view/113/113

Grouping Mixed Documents: Mexico Job Offers Case Study

Moreno Galván Elizabeth[(⊠)] ⓘ, Miguel Félix Mata Rivera ⓘ,
and Carmona García Enrique Alfonso ⓘ

UPIITA-IPN, Av. Instituto Politécnico Nacional 258, 07340 Gustavo A. Madero,
Mexico City, Mexico
elizabeth.moreno.galvan.05@gmail.com

Abstract. A mixed dataset is composed of structured and unstructured documents whose heterogeneous data formats complicate not only their processing but also their content analysis. Finding the semantic correspondence among documents stored in a mixed dataset requires identifying, combining, and assembling diverse techniques from many knowledge fields to analyze and reveal possible patterns among them. In the case of text documents, it has been addressed by processing semantic properties and linguistic relationships between words through vector representations and word embedding models. In this paper, we present a methodology to calculate the content proximity in mixed documents, using three techniques: similarity measure, doc2vec embedding model, cosine similarity, and K-means algorithm. The study is centered on the Mexican job market documents to find relationships among mixed documents of job offers. The results show that creating groupings of mixed documents, based on their semantic and cosine similarity, allows them to reveal patterns.

Keywords: Text classification · Mixed dataset · Embedding model · Similarity · doc2vec · K-means · Cosine similarity · Job offer · Vector space model

1 Introduction

Document similarity is a Natural Language Processing NLP [1] technique that has been widely used in various applications such as text classification [2], document semantic similarity detection [3, 4], authorship identification [5], information retrieval (IR) [6], answer questions chatbots [7], text summarization [8], sentiment analysis [9, 10] and applied in other complex study areas like medical or educational to name a few. In labor market area, employers spend great time writing and publishing available jobs information into text documents called job offers in order to find the most suitable professionals whose meet all the requirements needed. In this sense, the job offer is a mixed text document which is formed by structured and unstructured information. To find the correspondence among documents stored in such mixed dataset implies discover associations and patterns, also by clustering and classification. In this sense, what motivates this work is to report experiments applying the combined used of data analysis techniques, to make useful inferences about document similarity problem.

M. F. Mata-Rivera et al. (Eds.): GIS LATAM 2020, CCIS 1276, pp. 151–159, 2020.
https://doi.org/10.1007/978-3-030-59872-3_11

2 Literature Review

Writing a text document that meets some objective, for example a letter or research article is a common task. In some cases comparing such documents with others has become a necessary activity, such as authorship checking or find similar documents to be consulted and referenced in an research. At present, these processes are hindered due to the large number of documents available thanks to digital means, so carrying out search and consultation activities involves exhaustive work too complex to be carried out by a human being. That is why grouping, classifying and find correspondences among text documents, based on content analysis and the measurement of similarities between them, is a task that have been addressed by processing semantic properties and linguistic relationships between words present into documents. In this sense, several techniques have been proposed that can be grouped into two main categories [11]: content-based and knowledge-enriched based:

In the first group, the most used method is the Vector Space Model VSM [12], where each document is represented as a m-dimensional weighted vector and the dimensions correspond to individual characteristics or terms. The result is called the bag-of-words model. The limitation of this model is that it does not take into account polysemy (the same word can have multiple meanings) and synonymy (two words can represent the same concept).

The second group, includes Latent Semantic Analysis (LSA) [13], used to extract a latent semantic structure in documents by applying the reduction of dimensionality to the matrix of term – document. In the same group, Embedding Words, as word2vec [4, 14–18], is a technique that learns to read enormous amounts of texts and memorize which words seem to be similar in different contexts. An analogous method, also known as document embeddings Paragraph Vector or Doc2Vec [17], was presented by the same word2vec author, T. Mikolov [18], which represents documents as fixed-length, low-dimensionality vectors. Regarding unsupervised learning applied with Processing Natural Language NLP, there is a wide preference to apply K-Means technique [19–22] clearly stands out since several algorithms, both unsupervised and supervised, require that the text be preprocessed within the vector space, also implementing techniques such as bag of words, in addition to the use of other more such as binarization, tokenization, linguistic analysis and stemming.

As has been showed, the main difference between those techniques is that the first group uses only textual information contained within documents, while the second group enriches these documents by extracting information from other sources, usually knowledge bases.

3 Data Collection

The data was extracted from words that correspond to a job offers for some common professions such as Doctor, Lawyer, Secretary or Business Management. A total of 10,682 job offer records were collected from the Linkedin job search platform website. The dataset consists of all job offers published in spanish, with location in Mexico City. Table 1 describes the general structure of the dataset.

Table 1. Linkedin document sections.

Section	Description	Structured
Título	Job title offered	Yes
Empleador	Company name	Yes
Ubicación	Workplace	Yes
Descripción	Job offer details such as salary, schedule, requirements or functions	No
Nivel de experiencia	Experience Level: Prácticas/Sin Experiencia/Algo de responsabilidad/etc.	Yes
Tipo de empleo	Workday: Jornada completa/Medio tiempo	Yes
Función Laboral	Job function: Desarrollo empresarial/Ventas/Gestión de proyectos/Tecnologías de la Información/Consultoría/Ingeniería/, etc.	Yes
Sectores	Business sector: Alimentación y bebidas/Recursos Humanos/Ventas al por menor/Telecomunicaciones/Contabilidad/, etc.	Yes

4 Materials and Methods

4.1 Methodology

Based on the KDD methodology which has been widely used for data analysis, the applied methodology parts of the conception that there are groups of mixed documents available on the social network, thus consists of three main phases subdivided into phases ranging from 1) data collection to conform the experimental data warehouse, 2) pre-processing phase applying natural language techniques, for later apply analysis and also grouping techniques, and finally 3) present the results obtained which will show the possibility of grouping mixed text documents.

By this method, shown in Fig. 1 the resulting analysis will be obtained from the application of statistical, analytical, NLP, machine learning and data mining tools, and the generation of visualization models that help illustrate the value of information, making it a valuable resource for creation of business strategies.

The methodology description is resumed as follows:

4.2 Phase 1 Collection and Storage

To the conformation of the dataset, since obtaining data from the social media, the data source must have the property of being mixed, since as mentioned above, the treatment and combination of applied techniques is focused on this type of document. In this way, every document characteristic such as title, is stored as a study dimension.

Collection and storage   Processing and analysis   Results presentation

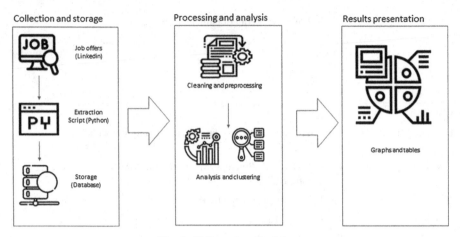

Fig. 1. Followed methodology.

4.3 Phase 2 Processing and Analysis

The computational treatment of textual information involves a mathematical modeling process and the use of paragraph embeddings technique, in which the texts are treated as objects and the words are represented in the vector space. Once the VSM has been obtained, it is possible to perform operations such as finding similarities between the vector representations by applying techniques such as calculating distances by cosine similarity [18] (see Fig. 2).

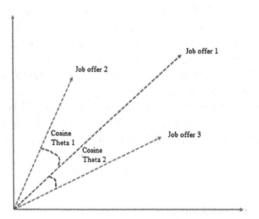

Fig. 2. Vectorial representations of job offers

The technique for grouping job offer documents proposed in this methodology is the K-means algorithm [9], one of the most widely used non-hierarchical cluster methods, which divides existing data into one or more clusters.

4.4   Phase 3 Results Presentation

To present the grouping results from the combined application of content analysis techniques, the representation was chosen by dispersion diagrams with colors that graphically support the distinction of the groups obtained and the differences between them obtained from each exploration.

5   Results

In order to carry out the documents grouping and classification, two experiments were carried out: grouping job offers by cosine similarity and grouping by K-Means algorithm.

5.1   Grouping Job Offers by Cosine Similarity

The corpus of documents corresponding to job offers from various fields was divided into training (70%) and test sets (30%). Thus, the model was trained with 7153 records in 100 epochs, with a window of 10 words. Later, to verify that it has learned all the words and if they have a contextual meaning, the search for the words "Sales", "Medical" and "Lawyer" was carried out, whose scatter plots are shown in Fig. 3 showing all the documents that are close or similar to the test documents contextually.

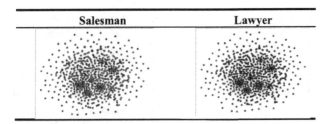

Fig. 3. Similarity between job offer documents by doc2vec testing model

From the doc2vec model, a *corpus* of job offer documents were compared one by one with the rest of the *corpus* using the cosine similarity formula 1.

$$similarity = cos\,\theta = A \cdot B \big/ ||A||\,||B|| = \frac{\sum_{i=1}^{n} A_i B_i}{\sqrt{\sum_{i=1}^{n} A_i^2}\sqrt{\sum_{i=1}^{n} B_i^2}} \tag{1}$$

Since the similarity score is between 0 or 1, a minimum threshold can be set such as 0.6, in this way similar document sets were created with a similarity score of any pair greater than 0.6.

A pair of experiments where applied:

i)   In the first experiment, it has been obtained a word2vec model, in which, the records were grouped from all the words contained in the dataset and its corresponding context.

ii) The second experiment consists in the application of doc2vec model, Fig. 4 shows a fragment of the set of similar documents obtained through the calculation of the 60% cosine similarity of a document (id: 369), using the doc2Vec trained model.

```
Document [369]: descriptionotorgaraltacalidadservicioiniciorepresentantebilingüecréditocobranzaaseráasequipoprofesionalesdedicadosmantenerolle
Similitud > 60%

Id: 643 = corporativogayossosolicitaexpansioncerradorventascomisionestopadascerradorencargacoordinarequipoagendadoresacudircitasconcretarve
Id: 257 = descripciónofertaintegrateequipoimportantempresaramosolicitagerenteoperacionescallcenteráreaatenciónclienteventasliderazgocaract
Id: 461 = ejecutivocallcenterventasdescripciónatenciónventatelefónicacllientessolicitaninformacióncampañafarmacéuticarequisitosexperienciaca
Id: 343 = requisitosdescripciónplazancallcentersalescenterempresalidercallcenterbúsquedaoperadorestelefónicosedadañospreparatoriatruncaconc
Id: 237 = idealpromotoriabúsquedacoordinadorrelacioneslaboralesdirectamenteaplicardebescumplirperfiledadañossexcindistintoescolaridadlicenc
Id: 637 = corporativogayossosolicitaexpansioncerradorventascomisionestopadascerradorencargacoordinarequipoagendadoresacudircitasconcretarve
Id: 276 = elaboraciónreportesestadisticasactividadesadministrativasmostrar ;
Id: 653 = necesitasdescripciónplazanúnetecallcenteroperadortelefónicolaborarcasarolanhorariostienesexperienciaejecutivotelefónicocampañaven
Id: 755 = ejecutivocallcentergeppempresadesarrolloportafoliomarcaasliderespresencianivelnacionalcolaboradoresinvitaformarfamiliaejecutivotel
Id: 34 = importantempresaramotelecomunicacionessolicitaabogadoregulatoriorequisitosinteresadoscubranperfilenviaractualizadodireccióncorreo
Id: 99 = descripciónofertamueblesaméricasolicitagestorcobranzaextrajudicialindispensablecontarautomóvilcilindrosmotocicletaresponsablegesti
Id: 104 = requerimospersonalcomprometidobrindarserviciosexcelentecalidadinteresadosdesarrollarsecrecerprofesionalmenteintegrándoseempresaab
Id: 353 = solicitamospersonalcontratacióninmediatadirectaofrecemossueldobaseprestacionesutilidadesgananciastopadasrenovacionespagadasquince
Id: 709 = massmarketscustomerserviceremoteimprovescustomersatisfactionsupportsalesprocesshandleoutboundsalesinquiriestakeincomingcustomerse
```

Fig. 4. Fragment of a list of documents similar to a job offer

Table 2 summarizes the groupings obtained as a result from both experiments whose cosine similarity calculation was greater than 60% (0.6).

Table 2. Groups by cosine similarity over 60%.

Embedding technique	Similarity score	Groups formed	Score of records inside each group	Dataset length
Word2Vec	60%–65%	255	20–30	10 682
Word2Vec	66%	1671	4	10 682
Word2Vec	Over 67% to 70%	7	3–4	10 682
Doc2Vec	60%	14	70–245	3311
Doc2Vec	60%	328	25–89	7153

Table 2 exemplifies that by doc2vec embedding model, the documents can be classified more effectively than by word2vec embedding model.

5.2 Grouping by K-Means Algorithm

Through this experiment, a training set from the *corpus* of job offers was modeled by the word2vec vector model. After the K-means algorithm application was produced the scatter plot in Fig. 5.

The graph shows that the words contained in job offer documents are very similar in context, so this method does not offer groupings that allow any representative distinction to be made between them.

On the other hand, an experiment where a set of the of job offers *corpus* were trained by doc2vec vector model and grouped using the K-means algorithm produces the Fig. 6 scatter plot.

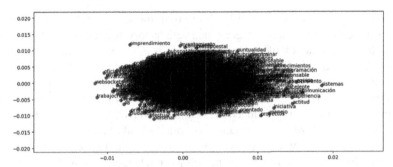

Fig. 5. Fragment of a list of documents similar to a job offer

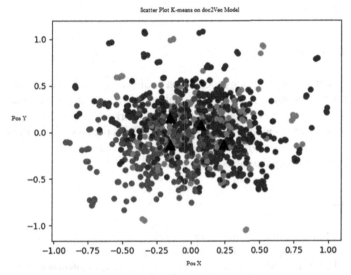

Fig. 6. Clustering by K-means algorithm application on doc2vec modeled set

As it can be observed, document sets have been obtained keeping some relation to each other, so it is possible to detect constant associations between documents.

6   Conclusions

In this paper, a methodology to explore job market in Mexico has been presented. emphasis is placed on focusing the study on detecting the causes of the phenomenon beyond the statistical approach. In this sense, the difficult in the analysis of documents from de job market such as job offers, lies in that the documents are not structured. To support the study of datasets containing this kind of documents, the document embedding model has been a recent technique, but that has shown visible advantages for content analysis and the detection of semantic relationships between documents, therefore, throughout this work some of the classic techniques of classification and text preprocessing have been proved within embedding models.

Experiments shown the great difficult to group the job offer documents from the word2vec model, since it has not generated satisfactory results, because it has been detected that within the job offer documents there is a common terminology, with few differentiators making it difficult to distinguish between them. However, to group the same documents from the doc2vec model, has given very good results allowing clustering by both proved techniques: cosine similarity and k-means, which means it is possible to create groups from similarity founded in documents no matter their mixed nature.

On the other hand, when it is required to work with other types of associated documents, such as resumes, which are used by recruiters to find the best candidate for the job offered, the problem of finding the person-job relationship is based on that there is no categorization, standardization or regulation that defines what the characteristics of a job offer are and this study opens up a study area that can help the adequate construction of these documents.

7 Future Work

The development of a methodology focused on finding correspondence, associations and patterns between job offers is proposed to determine if there is any grouping criterion by measuring similarity between them. To this end, work will be carried out on a greater number of experiments and analyzes, such as candidates profiles and relations between both, job offers and profiles with the expectation of impacting in a multidisciplinary way on the social and economic aspects of Mexico.

References

1. Oghbaie, M., Mohammadi Zanjireh, M.: Pairwise document similarity measure based on present term set. J. Big Data 5(1), 1–23 (2018). https://doi.org/10.1186/s40537-018-0163-2
2. Aldrin, F.J., Zapata, C.M., Isaza, F.A.: Una Propuesta para la Asistencia al Proceso de Interpretación de Textos utilizando Técnicas de Procesamiento del Lenguaje Natural e Ingeniería de Software. In: Avances en Sistemas e Informática Proceedings, vol. 4, no.3, Medellín, ISSN 1657-7663 (2007)
3. Palmer, Z., Wu, M.: Verbs semantics and lexical selection. In: Proceedings of the 32nd Annual Meeting on Association for Computational Linguistics, pp. 133–138. Association for Computational Linguistics (1994)
4. Elekes, A., Englhardt, A., Schäler, M., Böhm, K.: Toward meaningful notions of similarity in NLP embedding models. Int. J. Digit. Libr. 21, 109–128 (2020). Springer-Verlag GmbH Germany, part of Springer Nature (2018)
5. Rozi, F., Sukmana, F.: Document grouping by using meronyms and type-2 fuzzy association rule mining. J. ICT Res. Appl. 11(3), 268–283 (2017)
6. Alonso, I., Contreras, D.: Evaluation of semantic similarity metrics applied to the automatic retrieval of medical documents: An UMLS approach. Expert Syst. Appl. 44, 386–399 (2016)
7. Robert, D.: The return of the chatbots. Nat. Lang. Eng. 22(5), 811–817 (2016). Cambridge
8. Mutlu, B., Sezer, E.A., Akcayol, M.A.: Multi-document extractive text summarization: A comparative assessment on features. Knowl.-Based Syst. 183, 104848 (2019)
9. Vilares, D., Gómez, C., Alonso, M.A.: Universal, unsupervised (rule-based), uncovered sentiment analysis. Knowl.-Based Syst. 118, 45–55 (2017)

10. Wu, Z., Palmer, M.: Verbs semantics and lexical selection. In: Proceedings of the 32nd Annual Meeting on Association for Computational Linguistics, pp. 133–138. Association for Computational Linguistics (1994)
11. Benedett, F., Beneventano, D., Bergamaschi, S., Simonini, G.: Computing inter-document similarity with Context Semantic Analysis. Elsevier Inf. Syst. **80**, 136–147 (2019)
12. Sidorov, G.: Syntactic n-grams in Computational Linguistics, pp. pp. 5–19. Springer, Cham (2019)
13. Botana, G.: La técnica del Análisis de la Semántica Latente (LSA/LSI) como modelo informático de la comprensión del texto y el discurso, Tesis Doctoral, U. Autónoma de Madrid (2010)
14. Rezaeinia, S.M., Rahmania, R., Ghods, A., Veisi, H.: Sentiment analysis based on improved pre-trained word embeddings. Expert Syst. Appl. **117**, 139–147 (2019)
15. Nguyen, H.T., Duong, P.H., Cambria, E.: Learning short-text semantic similarity with word embeddings and external knowledge sources. Knowl.-Based Syst. **182**, 104842 (2019). Elsevier
16. Church, W.K.: Emerging trends: Word2Vec. Nat. Lang. Eng. **23**(1), 155–162 (2017)
17. Markov, I., Gómez-Adorno, H., Posadas-Durán, J.-P., Sidorov, G., Gelbukh, A.: Author profiling with Doc2vec neural network-based document embeddings. In: Pichardo-Lagunas, O., Miranda-Jiménez, S. (eds.) MICAI 2016. LNCS (LNAI), vol. 10062, pp. 117–131. Springer, Cham (2017). https://doi.org/10.1007/978-3-319-62428-0_9
18. Quoc, V.L., Mikolov, T.: Distributed Representations of Sentences and Documents. Google Inc., Mountain View (2014)
19. Usino, W., Prabuwono, A.S., Hamed, K., Allehaibi, S., Bramantoro, A., Hasniaty, A., Amaldi, W.: Document similarity detection using k-means and cosine distance. Int. J. Adv. Comput. Sci. Appl. (IJACSA) **10**(2) (2019)
20. Singh, A., Rose, C., Visweswariah, K., Chenthamarakshan, Y., Kambhatla, N.: Prospect: a system for screening candIdates for recruItment. In: Proceedings of the 19th ACM International Conference on Information and Knowledge Managementpp, pp. 659–668. ACM, (2010)
21. Li, Y., Tripathi, A., Srinivasan, A.: Challenges in Short Text Classification: The Case of Online Auction Disclosure. Association for Information Systems, AIS Electronic Library (AISeL) (2016)
22. Kumar, A., Pandey, A., Kaushik, S.: Machine learning methods for solving complex ranking and sorting issues in human resourcing. In: IEEE 7th International Advance Computing Conference (2017)

Author Index

Printed in the United States
By Bookmasters